Some authors write about the "latest sec[...] this book Kim shares how you can practically implement secrets that have stood the test of time. Reading this book is like sitting with a trusted friend or your own personal marriage mentor and gleaning from their years of experience. Your relationship will be better for having done so.

—**Ron L. Deal**
Bestselling author of *The Smart Stepfamily*
and *Dating and the Single Parent*

In a world where many marriages struggle, Dr. Kim's book is a catalyst for change. As you learn these seven secrets and apply them to your marriage, you open the door for marriage blessings from God that you never imagined were possible.

—**Herbert Cooper**
Senior Pastor, People's Church in Oklahoma
Author of *But God Changes Everything*

When I found out Dr. Kimberling was releasing this book, I began praying that it would land in the hands of thousands of people simply because there is no one I know who speaks greater wisdom into the area of relationships than Kim. He has years of wisdom and experience that can help people who are married, engaged, dating, or hopeful. What a gift this book is to the church and to the world!

—**Dr. Clayton King**
President of Crossroads Summer Camps and Crossroads Missions
Teaching Pastor, NewSpring Church in South Carolina
Distinguished Professor of Evangelism, Anderson University

I have known Kim and Nancy for over 10 years and have seen the 7 secrets at work firsthand. They have an awesome marriage. You too can have an awesome marriage, but it takes work and a few secrets tucked away in God's Word that Dr. Kimberling will bring to light in this amazing new resource for couples.

—**Rodney Cox**
Founder/President, Ministry Insights

7 SECRETS
TO AN
AWESOME
MARRIAGE

Strengthen Your Most
Intimate Relationship

KIM KIMBERLING, PHD

ZONDERVAN

7 Secrets to an Awesome Marriage
Copyright © 2015 by Kim Kimberling, Ph.D.

This title is also available as a Zondervan ebook. Visit www.zondervan.com/ebooks.

Requests for information should be addressed to:
Zondervan, 3900 *Sparks Drive SE, Grand Rapids, Michigan 49546*

Library of Congress Cataloging-in-Publication Data

Kimberling, Kim.
    7 secrets to an awesome marriage / Kim Kimberling, PhD. — 1 [edition].
      pages cm
    Includes bibliographical references and index.
    ISBN 978-0-310-34227-4 (softcover : alk. paper)
    1. Marriage – Religious aspects – Christianity. I. Title. II. Title: Seven secrets
to an awesome marriage.
    BV835.K5425 2015
    248.8'44 – dc23   2015015498

Published in association with the literary agency of Hudson Bible.

Cover design: Dual Identity
Cover photo: Geoff Duncan / Lightstock.com®
Interior design: Kait Lamphere

First printing May 2015 / Printed in the United States of America

This book is dedicated to my Mom and Dad.
For fifty-seven years they were my living blueprint
of what an Awesome Marriage is all about.

CONTENTS

FOREWORD

If someone told you that you had a 50 percent chance of losing all your money by the end of the month, we are certain they would have your full attention. You'd be asking questions, digging deeper, doing everything possible to make sure you ended up on the right side of those odds. Or imagine if a trusted mechanic explained you could very likely be killed in a car wreck if you don't replace your brakes. There is no doubt that you'd think twice about speeding down the highway without making the appropriate repairs. And if someone told you there is a 50 percent chance one of your children would be kidnapped if you dropped him or her off at the mall without supervision, you know your kid would never visit the mall alone again.

Knowing there is a good chance of some life-altering tragedy, you would do everything you could to avoid it. And yet, every day people get married with full knowledge that approximately 50 percent of marriages end in divorce. So why don't we do everything we can to take the odds seriously? Even though many marriages don't make it and others just barely limp along, it doesn't have to be that way for you.

Sound wisdom and smart preparation can make all the difference. That's why Amy and I are so thankful for Dr. Kimberling's practical, deeply spiritual, and game-changing book. I'm honored to serve as Dr. Kimberling's pastor and have the blessing of knowing him both personally and professionally. He and his wife, Nancy, are not only incredible servants, but also world-class teachers. I have lost count of all the struggling marriages our church has sent to the Kimberlings in desperate need of help. Time and time again, God has used this family to save marriages and build God-honoring homes.

Amy and I won't promise you that an awesome marriage is easy — but we will assure you that it's possible. And Dr. Kimberling will walk you step-by-step through seven very doable practices that will help you have the marriage you've always dreamed of having. With these seven secrets, along with a wholehearted commitment to Christ and to each other, you can and will have an awesome marriage.

—*Craig and Amy Groeschel*

A FIRST WORD

If I was twenty again and in love and ready to get married, I would be scared to death. The world often makes this whole marriage thing to look like a catastrophe waiting to happen, and I am not sure I would want to take the risk. I would be looking around for other options, which is exactly what a bunch of people are doing today. Cohabit, date a bunch of different people, do not commit to anyone, and/or stay single forever.

I could have bought into that. I might have wanted to play it safe. This marriage thing might have been conventional once, but now, it must be for daredevils or crazy people.

Let's be honest: the statistics don't look so good. Nor do the stories we hear from those we know and love whose marriages have failed.

Yet even with all the negative things about marriage today, my real bottom line is this: I love being married. Nancy and I started dating during our college years. She was eighteen and I was twenty. We loved dating. On campus I would wait outside her class until it ended so I could walk her to the next one. We ate our meals together, studied together, and talked on the phone way too late each night. It was an adventure for us. We were in college and having a blast. We had friends, we had fun, and we had each other.

Our relationship grew to the point that two years later we bungee-jumped into marriage. Nancy was finishing college and I was working full time. Our first apartment was brand new. Not only were we the first people to live in it, but we were also the first to watch it literally fall apart around us. So much for the "if it is new, you won't have problems with it" philosophy. With my first job, I made enough money to pay the bills, but there was very little extra. We had lots of creative date nights. Our favorite centered around watching the sunset and the sailboats while sitting on the dam of a lake close to where we lived. It was magical for us.

Right out of the starting blocks, we had no idea what we were doing, but we were committed to each other and to this marriage. We had ups and downs and almost crashed and burned a few times, but we hung in there. And you know what? All these years later, we would do it all over again. We would go over the hills and through the valleys and relive the good days and the bad days because we have a different perspective today.

We can now see how all those things we encountered over the years knit us together. We see that God had this plan for us and never took His hand away. Sure, there were times we did not think He was there, but looking back, He was, and today we have this incredibly Awesome Marriage. It took time and it took work and it was exhausting, but it was worth it.

So here is what bothers me about this growing negative attitude toward marriage. I am afraid people will be scared away from marrying. I am afraid married people will give up because everybody else is giving up. The sad thing to me is that if people never marry or if they easily give up, they relinquish their chance of ever having what God has given Nancy and me. God has a plan for marriage and for your marriage, and that plan is not just pretty good. It is awesome.

Set aside those other stats that scare you. Turn your back on the stats that say marriage cannot work, and take a chance. Why? Because if you take the chance on marriage according to God's way, I'm fully convinced you'll be happily surprised. Sure, there are risks, but I believe with everything I have that the risks are truly worth taking.

Nancy and I took the risk. We began our life together like most young couples today. We had no idea what we were doing, but that was okay because we had a God that did. Even though the ride has not been perfect, neither one of us has ever regretted taking that risk. The upside is just too rewarding for you to miss the opportunity.

Let's begin looking at seven secrets that will give you an awesome marriage—the kind of marriage God had in mind from the start. You are going to meet a number of people and hear their stories. Some are willing to embrace the secrets and some are not. Some of them fly and some of them crash. You can decide for yourself what you think will work for you.

STOP

The Insanities That Hold Us Back

"Doing the same thing over and over and expecting different results"—this is the textbook definition of insanity. Most of us don't consider ourselves insane, of course, yet this is the exact pattern we often act out in our relationships. And that's where the real problems begin.

The insanities we bring into our relationships, of course, don't just arise out of the blue. They all have roots. Some roots are more difficult to get rid of than others. In fact, many of the roots grow out of our family of origin. But no matter the source of our insanities, they seem to keep us from following God's plan for marriage. That is the greatest insanity of all.

The longer we have practiced our insanities, the more difficult it is to break free of them. Whether you are young or not so young, married, divorced, widowed, single, or whatever, the odds are pretty good that you have an insanity or two that needs to be addressed. If you choose to deal with the skewed way of thinking, life gets better and relationships can get a lot better. If you choose to not deal with it, then . . .

Meet Richard and Lisa. Richard just turned forty. Lisa is thirty-five. Today they are married. Tomorrow, who knows? This is the third time Richard has been married, and he is sure it will also be his third divorce. Same for Lisa. People come to my office for a number of reasons. Some have hope that things can get better, and often they do. Some come to counseling so they can tell family and friends that they tried "everything" before giving in to divorce. I was pretty sure that Richard and Lisa were in the latter category. Visiting the counselor's office was the last thing on their list that needed to be checked off. I listened as they unfolded their stories.

Richard grew up in a divorced home. He was the oldest of three kids, and from the time he was eight he was the "man of the house." His mom worked long hours to support the family, and his dad just disappeared. Richard had no model of what it took to be a dad, a husband, and a man. He was forced to figure that out on his own. He took a paper route at the age of twelve, and by the time he was sixteen he worked a full-time job.

> It was easy for Richard to believe that he just married the wrong person the first time. But he never took the time to look within himself and see what needed to change.

At seventeen, he fell in love, and the summer he graduated from high school he walked down the aisle for the first time. It seemed the right thing to do. They were in love, they both had jobs, they rented a little apartment, and they both planned to start at the junior college in town in the fall. But by September, she was pregnant. Her pregnancy was rough. They began to fight a lot, money was tight, and by Christmas she had moved back in with her parents. Richard never lived a day in the same house as his son. Marriage number one.

Like many of us, it was easy for Richard to believe that he just married the wrong person the first time. But he never took the time to look within himself and see what needed to change. Richard was doing the same thing again and expecting a different result. Insanity. He took his time and at twenty-three met the love of his life. They worked in the same office. She was a year younger and had never been married. She wanted a strong man, and Richard seemed to fit the profile.

They dated almost a year, and at the age of twenty-four Richard entered his second try at marriage. He was sure that this one would work. Both had good jobs, they bought a house together, and the first year was like a love story right out of Hollywood. It was fifteen months before they had their first fight and, according to Richard, they made up for lost time. In his first marriage, when the conflict began, the marriage ended. Richard was determined it would not be that way this time. He was not giving up and would not let her give up either.

For seven years they lived a roller-coaster life of peace and chaos — a few days of bliss and then a day or two of fighting. But they never learned how to resolve conflict, and that was their biggest problem. So the same issues returned over and over. It was similar to marriage number one but on repeat for a much longer period of time. Finally the days of conflict dominated their calendar, and they agreed to part ways. Marriage number two.

Richard said he then went through a period of soul searching. He asked himself questions. "What happened?" "What went wrong this time?" Yet he walked through this process alone, without wise friends or a counselor. Finally, he came to the same conclusion he had for marriage one: he had married the wrong person, again.

Still, maybe he needed to try church, he thought. It could not do any harm, and he just might meet the right woman. Richard began church shopping and finally settled on one that had a good singles program. Richard's definition of a "good singles program" was one with plenty of attractive, eligible women.

Richard had been in the church a little over a year when Lisa walked in one day. He could not take his eyes off her. Now it all made sense. He had married the wrong woman — twice! They began to date and over the next eighteen months did everything the church asked them to do to prepare for marriage. Richard admitted that he was just going through the motions of what the church asked them to do. Lisa was the right one for him and that was all that mattered. This was different because he had found the one. At the age of thirty-four, Richard walked down the aisle for the third time.

As he stood at the front of the church, Lisa walked down the aisle to meet him. Richard thought how beautiful she was and how she was different from the others, but he had no idea that Lisa was bringing some baggage of her own.

Lisa's Story

Lisa loved her dad. She had an older brother and an older sister, but there was no doubt in anyone's mind that Lisa was his favorite — hands down, the favorite. With her dad giving most of his attention to Lisa, her mom tried to make up the void to her siblings. It almost became a game. Which parent could outdo the other?

In Lisa's eyes, her dad won and her parents' marriage lost. They never openly fought, but their marriage was not much of a partnership, either. They never divorced, but a repeat of her parents' marriage was not something Lisa wanted. As a result, Lisa's role model of a wife, mother, and a woman was tainted. She never really had a relationship with her mother as she grew up, and now as adults their relationship was worse than ever.

After college, Lisa focused on building her career. Marriage was not appealing in Lisa's eyes. She seldom dated because she simply did not have time for those relationships, or so she told herself. At the age of twenty-eight she began to panic as the reality of her life hit her head-on. She was getting older, and in the back of her mind she knew that at some point in life she wanted children. It was now time to begin that quest.

Lisa did not worry about her past. Sure, her family was dysfunctional, but that was a long time ago. She was way past those issues. Now she was successful in her work, confident and attractive, and focused on what she wanted.

A friend introduced her to Dustin and they really hit it off. He treated her well—just like her dad had. Four months of dating later, and they were planning a private, romantic destination wedding—with just the two of them. But the romance began to fade as soon as they boarded their plane home—that was when Mr. Wonderful began to change. At thirty thousand feet, he outlined his list of expectations of her, including what she could and could not do. Lisa was shocked but said nothing at first. Eight weeks later, she could not take it any longer. She moved out and filed for divorce. Marriage number one was over.

A friend suggested a support group for people going through divorce. Lisa agreed to go, but she felt out of place. Most of these people had been married for at least a few years. Her marriage had lasted a few weeks. Sticking it out was difficult, but the final night of the support group came. Coffee and cookies were served after the meeting, and she decided to stick around for a few minutes. In those few minutes, she met her second husband. He was almost perfect and totally understood her. After all, they had been through the same thing.

They began a nine-month dating relationship. Marriage number two.

On the plane ride home from their honeymoon, there was no list of expectations. Lisa knew this marriage was different, and for a while it was. The honeymoon phase lasted almost a year, and even though some of the romance began to fade, Lisa was happy.

For Lisa, the next couple of years were a blur. Her husband was placed on the "fast track" at his job. The demands on him and his time were great, but so were the rewards. Lisa liked the rewards at first. She always drove a new car and was living in her dream house, but rewards without a husband there to enjoy them with her was not what she wanted in a marriage. The times they were together were marred by fighting. They grew further and further apart, and one day Lisa was done. Marriage number two ended just like marriage number one.

Lisa was devastated. What was wrong? All she wanted was a happy marriage. Was that too much to ask? She talked to a friend at work who was also divorced. The friend invited her to church. She wanted Lisa to go to the singles class with her. Lisa was reluctant. Walking into a room full of singles scared her, and she had never been big on the whole church idea. After weeks of saying no, Lisa finally said yes.

Lisa was really not sure what she was looking for in the class. Maybe community or new friends or just a safe place to be. Her plan was to give it three or four weeks and then, if none of those were happening, to gracefully bow out.

Lisa may have looked calm on the outside that first week, but on the inside she was scared to death. It was like her first high school dance all over again. Maybe even worse. Week two was better, and by the time week three rolled around she had no anxiety and was getting bored with the whole thing. The people were nice, but she was not attracted to any of the men. The lessons were probably okay, but she did not listen well. Not telling her friend, she made up her mind that Sunday number four would be her last.

That fourth Sunday morning brought no anxious feelings. This was just a routine that she was getting ready to break. She spent little time picking out what to wear, putting on her makeup, and fixing her hair. Why bother? Nothing was going to change. She left the house late and was ready to get this over with.

The class had already started when Lisa walked in. Fortunately, her friend had saved her a seat. As she scanned the room, her gaze stopped on someone new. She nudged her friend and asked if she knew the new guy. Lisa found out that the guy was not new. His name was Richard, and he had been out of town the past few weeks. Lisa thought to herself, "Miracles do happen." As the lesson ended, Lisa slipped out to the restroom to freshen her makeup and redo her hair. As she walked back in, she ran into

Richard—literally! They laughed and talked and went to lunch together. This was the guy. She knew it deep inside.

Lisa's version of their dating relationship mirrored Richard's except that she took seriously the instruction the church offered them as they prepared for marriage. She assumed Richard was taking it just as seriously. The wedding was wonderful, and all their church friends attended. This marriage would be different. Lisa had learned from her mistakes and knew what to do and what not to do.

For almost two years she put into practice all the things she had learned to make marriages work. Then Richard changed. It was almost an overnight change. Where did the Richard she had fallen in love with go? He was short with her, and his words were often terse. She remembered thinking that she had never seen him angry, and now she seldom saw him when he was not. She took it for a long time and finally started fighting back. The fights got ugly and Lisa was done. Really done. More done than marriage number two.

Two Choices

As Lisa finished her story, they both turned to look at me. I was not sure what they were thinking, but I thought it was along the lines of, "We know our marriage is hopeless. Just confirm that for us, and we will get out of here."

I sat there a long time without saying anything. Silence is difficult for most of us, and this was certainly true of Richard and Lisa. They began to squirm a little. I was not playing a game with them. I wanted them to really hear what I was going to say. It would not be a lecture. It would not be a confirmation of their hopeless situation. Instead, it would be a challenge to both of them.

"As I see it, you have two choices. One choice is to divorce and move on with your lives. You do not have children, so that makes it easier for you because you will never have to see each other again. If you choose this option, my guess is that I will see you both again back here in a couple of years, each with a different mate. I believe you will just continue the pattern you are in of falling in love, getting married, and getting divorced. There is no reason to think that you will stop this insanity.

"You also have a second option. You can choose to make this marriage work. It will not be easy. It will take a lot of effort and a lot of time from each of you. In the end, I believe it is the only sensible thing to do. Together you can discover what building and living an awesome marriage is all about. The decision is yours."

As a counselor, my dream is to help couples say yes to the challenge of building a healthy marriage with joy and enthusiasm.

But Richard and Lisa just sat there. I had ruined their buzz. They were already mentally dividing up the furniture, the money, and the other possessions. Richard had signed up for an online dating service. I threw them a curve ball because I told them that I had hope.

I asked them to hold off doing anything for a week. During that time, I asked them to do a couple of things. First, I asked them to pray and seek God's guidance in this decision. Second, I asked them to talk to people who have good marriages and to ask them what they had done to get where they were today. Then I booked them a follow-up appointment. Richard and Lisa stood up, thanked me, shook my hand, and walked out of my office. I had no idea if I would ever see them again.

Facing Your Baggage

Richard and Lisa mirror many of the issues I see couples and individuals face today. Let's look at Richard first. By outward appearances at age seventeen, Richard looked pretty good. He was responsible, with a strong work ethic, good grades, and high hopes for life. Not a bad package. Yet as a husband he was a train wreck waiting to happen, and it did. Richard never had a dad as a model. What he learned about being a man and a husband he picked up from life experiences. That included TV, movies, his best friend's divorced dad, and an alcoholic uncle.

Richard searched for the right things in all the wrong places.

Then he was young—just seventeen on the day of his first marriage. Teen marriages are tough, and the statistics on them are not good. Granted, some couples make it, but they are the exception. I believe the final straw came when his first wife became pregnant. Here was this young couple trying to figure things out, starting college, and now adding parenting on top of it. The stress was great, the maturity was not there, and the marriage crashed.

That part of Richard's story is not uncommon. Many couples go into a first marriage with the odds stacked against them, and usually the odds win *unless*—and this is a big unless—they take the time to deal with the dysfunctions from their past.

The key to whether they will succeed is the next step because we usually do one of two things. Some people back up, get help, take a long look at themselves, and reinvent their thoughts and ideas of what it takes to have a successful marriage. Even though none of us wants to repeat unhealthy cycles, those habits and hangups do not just go away. We need to work and often to seek the guidance and wisdom of a pastor or Christian counselor to help guide us through the process. This then gives the opportunity to break any unhealthy cycles we may be in. That is how prospective couples may begin to prepare for marriage instead of preparing for divorce.

> **Some people back up, get help, take a long look at themselves, and reinvent their thoughts and ideas of what it takes to have a successful marriage.**

The other thing people usually do is basically nothing. Like Richard, they blame the failed marriage on marrying the wrong person. That makes the transition easier. They think, "I do not have to change. I just need to find the right person." Let me tell you how often I think that analysis works—never!

Lisa learned how to be a wife the same way that Richard learned how to be a husband: from TV, movies, and a few other people that she was around. She never gave it much thought because, when the time came, she would figure it out. After all, she was an intelligent woman.

Richard and Lisa did what far too many of us do today. We work hard, we get an education or learn a trade, we make money, we buy things, we have kids, and we think marriage will take care of itself. Then we are shocked when it does not. What if we put as much effort into our marriages as we did into our careers?

Let that soak in. Would our marriages be better? Would the divorce rate go down?

You see, just like Richard and Lisa, we have a choice. We can continue in our destructive patterns in marriage or we can choose to stop the insanity.

Our Newlywed Wake-Up Call

Looking back, we can often see God's hand at work in our lives in a way that we cannot in the middle of our circumstances. In high school, as a junior, I made an early decision to attend an out-of-state college after graduation. It seemed like a good choice. There were older guys I knew who attended the college and liked it.

My parents were on board as they wanted me to go out of state at least for the first year. Done. One problem that surfaced later with this decision was the fact that I never visited the school campus before my parents dropped me off at the beginning of my freshman year. By the time their car taillights faded in the distance, I was thinking that I had made a big mistake.

Having always been resilient, I decided I could make things work in this new situation. By the end of week one, my resilience was gone and I was sick—literally. I vomited in the bathroom and I vomited walking to class. I was never more miserable in my life, and I had no one to blame but myself.

Transferring schools went from an option to a necessity. My parents said yes, but not until the end of the semester. I spent six hours drawing a countdown calendar that I hung above my bed.

My roommate thought I was crazy, and he was close to being right. I was obsessed with leaving. The question was no longer when I would get to leave. It was where was I going. I was desperate.

My senior year in high school had brought a new out-of-state student to our school. We became friends, and he was headed to Texas Christian University in Fort Worth, Texas. Listening to him, I always thought TCU was a good choice. It was a perfect fit for him. Now it became my promised land. I enrolled for the second semester of my freshman year at TCU and walked on to my second college campus in five months.

Even though I made the same mistake with TCU that I did with college number one (my first day of school was the first time I stepped foot on the campus), I had a sense this would be different. I had a good friend there, and Fort Worth was a comfortable fit for me. It seemed more like home, and I was excited to be there.

As I began the second semester of my freshman year in college, Nancy was in her junior year of high school in Houston. As time grew closer to high school graduation, Nancy was headed to a large state university. As a courtesy to a friend, she also applied to TCU with no intention of going there. Two weeks before the start of her freshman year of college, Nancy made a bold, unexpected move and passed up the state school, instead heading to TCU. As my junior year began, I had no idea that my soul mate was now on the same campus with me.

By the middle of that year, I was pretty frustrated with the whole dating process. Far too many of my dating experiences had gone sour. I'd had lots of blind dates, but none ever worked out. I had a couple of decent relationships, but they were pretty short-lived. Halfway through my junior year, I decided to focus on schoolwork, hang out with my friends, and only date when I had to.

In February came my first "had to." There was a party, and everyone was going. I was facing a Saturday night alone when my roommate asked me one more time if he could "fix me up" with one of his girlfriend's friends. He had asked before, and I always said no. In my mind all blind dates were the same—bad. As the weekend got closer, in a weak moment, I finally said yes.

That Saturday night my life changed forever. As I sat in the freshman girls' dorm lobby waiting for my date to come down the elevator, my mind was on a lot of things besides the date. Having a date let me go to the party and not feel like some nerd who was there alone. Once we arrived I could hang with my friends, and she could hang with hers, and then I would take her back to the dorm. Great plan.

About that time the elevator door opened, and out walked Nancy. I am seldom at a loss for words, but at that time and in that place, I was. She was beautiful and had a smile that made my heart pound in my chest. I had no idea what was happening inside of me, but I liked it. That night I made a total fool of myself, and Nancy told my roommate's girlfriend that she never wanted to go out with me again. When I finally had a date with a girl who mesmerized me, I had blown it.

Now this is the part where things got interesting. Even though I would have done almost anything to have another chance with Nancy, for some reason, I let it go, and I never let it go. I wanted to call her, but I did not. I wanted to find out where her classes were and just "run into" her, but I did not. I wanted to ask her friends if they thought there was any chance, but I did not.

Then the miracle happened. Three weeks later she casually mentioned to her friend that for some reason she wanted to go out with me again. I jumped on the opportunity, and this time I was prepared. With the shock factor gone, I was determined to just be myself. If she liked me, I knew it would not be because I was trying to be someone that I was not. That successful second date became step one as we began our life together.

Dating and marriage are different. I tell people that all the time, but they often do not believe me. They think if they get along well while they are dating, they will get along even better in marriage. I thought the same thing, and after two years of dating we walked down the aisle. Perfect wedding. Perfect bride. Perfect everything.

Our first year was pretty normal even though we discovered that we had a lot of adjusting to do. It was just weird living with someone of the opposite sex. There are many things about the opposite sex that neither of you even thinks about going into marriage. If you are married, you get that, and if you are not, I am not about to burst your bubble here. Besides, Nancy's adjustments were by far greater than mine.

We lived in a small apartment, and it provided little space for privacy, which seemed to be more difficult for the wife than the husband. We shared a tiny bathroom, a tiny closet, and a ginormous king-size bed that almost filled our bedroom. The apartment was also beginning to fall apart. Doors were coming off their hinges, the kitchen cabinets began to sag, and the hood above the stove crashed down on top of our almost-ready dinner. Eventually we were able to graduate to a bigger apartment, but this is where we started out. Maybe your story is similar.

When you're dating, it's natural to focus on the ways you are so much alike. You bond through what you have in common. That was me. On the outside, I thought my family and Nancy's family were similar, but as we began married life together, I found out that they were not. No one ever talked to us about dysfunction. No one told us about differences. No one taught us how to communicate or fight. I had this brilliant belief that in marriage, sex solved everything. But as I quickly found out, this was not the case. This whole being married was a weird deal that was difficult for me to comprehend.

Our newlywed bliss shifted into a newlywed wake-up call—unlike anything I had ever expected. It confused me. I was living with my best friend, and I was crazy about her, but there were times I thought we were going to kill each other. Let the insanity begin.

The Insanity of Unrealistic Expectations

There are probably as many "insanities"—patterns of destructive habit we repeat over and over—as there are marriages. We all seem to have them. Mine may be different from yours, but they are still there.

And just like some of our insanities are rooted in our past and our family upbringing, others are rooted in our expectations of the future. So let's take a look at the expectations we bring to marriage. My mother, for example, was not perfect but was pretty close. That was not just my opinion. It seemed to be the opinion of most everyone that was ever around her. As I grew up, our home was the place all my friends wanted to be. Mom not only always had food to offer but also a listening ear. My friends loved talking to her. Often I would have friends over and find myself alone in my room as they made their way to the kitchen to spend time with my mom.

> **There are probably as many "insanities"—patterns of destructive habit we repeat over and over—as there are marriages.**

As I look back, I see that many of the skills I use as a counselor I learned from her. She listened well and gave wise counsel at the perfect time. She was a strong woman with a gentle spirit. As a wife, she let my dad lead, but he listened to her, and he valued her input. They were truly a team and deeply respected each other. This was my model, and I thought every home was pretty much like mine. That is what many of us do. The home we grew up in, right or wrong, was our first textbook of what marriage is or is not all about.

Nancy grew up in a fairly dysfunctional home with little security and lots of turmoil. Trusting was difficult for her. When we married, I wanted her to trust me and my decisions—that was my expectation. Nancy needed to be like my mother. Two problems came with this belief. Nancy was not my mother, and she was not going to just blindly follow anyone whether that person was her husband or not.

One of my biggest challenges came when I shared something with Nancy and she began asking questions. If I shared an idea, she asked questions. If I wanted us to do something, she asked questions. My expectation was that she would like and support my ideas and go along with the things I wanted us to do. Her questions made me feel like she was throwing cold water on everything I shared with her, and I would respond in anger.

It did not take long for me to realize that there was something deeply wrong. My problem was that I thought the wrong was with her. How could I be wrong? My family was perfect. The problem had to be with her. She is the one who came out of a mess.

So I began the process of trying to change her into the person I knew she needed to be. Have you ever tried to change a type A, smart, independent woman into anything? I didn't get it. How could she be refusing this opportunity that I was giving her? I thought I could lift her out of the pit, and we could have a great marriage just like my parents did.

It often amazes me as a counselor that I can clearly and usually quickly see the issues in my patients, but in my own life, it is like sometimes I am wearing blinders. Finally I took the blinders off and began to see the situation more objectively. I realized that I needed to do something different. (I can often be a very slow learner.) I was as much a part of our insanity as she was.

Many years into marriage, I was studying different ways people communicate and how that can affect a marriage. Nancy and I took an assessment that not only pointed out our differences but also gave us practical insight into how we could actually embrace these differences and grow our marriage. Finally, I understood. Nancy was not questioning my ideas or what I wanted to do. She was just trying to better understand what I was saying.

This was relationship-changing for us. My expectation had been unrealistic. Over and over I told her how much I wanted her to be on my side, and she said that is what she wanted, too. Yet, when I shared something, here came the questions. Now I understood. This wife that I thought was my adversary could be my biggest advocate. I just needed to take the time to answer her questions. Once she understood and her questions were answered, she was 100 percent on board.

Healthy Versus Unhealthy Expectations

When you hit pause to reevaluate your expectations, the effect can be exactly what it was for Nancy and me: relationship-changing. As you think about the word "expectations," what does it mean to you? The dictionary tells us that the word, a noun, is "a strong belief that something will happen or be the case in the future." Thus, applied to marriage, I think my spouse will respond or act in a particular way. Now that is not all bad.

When Nancy and I stood at the altar and were married, we made some commitments to each other and to God. The expectation that we would be faithful to each other was an outgrowth of those commitments. So were the expectations that we would stand by each other's side through trials like sickness and financial hardship. The expectation that I would work and provide for Nancy and our family was an expectation that we agreed on. We both had expectations of how we wanted to be treated and how we wanted to treat each other. These were good and mostly came from God's instructions in the Bible.

So there are many good, healthy expectations for a husband and a wife in a marriage.

Two of the keys in dealing with expectations are whether they are spoken or unspoken and whether they are realistic or unrealistic. If I have an expectation of Nancy and do not tell her what that expectation is and then get angry with her because she did not do it, is that fair? Of course not. Yet, how often do we do that in marriage? We expect our spouse to greet us with a kiss when we wake up in the morning. We expect our spouse to call or text us during the day to stay in touch. We expect our spouse to help around the house.

Now, none of those expectations are wrong. They are pretty healthy ones in a marriage today, but if I expect these and never share those expectations with my spouse, that is not fair. For example, if my expectation is for my spouse to contact me sometime during the day to show her love, and I do not tell her about this expectation, it is unfair if I get mad when she does not. Expectations need to be shared.

Some of our expectations are realistic and some are unrealistic. If Nancy expects me to provide for the family, that is realistic. If she expects me to provide multiple homes for us in exotic places around the world, that is unrealistic.

I know that is an extreme example, but you would be amazed at some of the unrealistic expectations I hear from people in the counseling room. One that I often hear is that their spouse is not meeting all their needs. The reality is that in God's design, He should meet certain needs in our lives, and then there are needs He will help our spouse to meet. If I have an expectation of Nancy, I need to share it. Then she can tell me if it is realistic or not.

Healthy expectations are good for a marriage. Unhealthy expectations can kill a marriage.

Action Step

Think about the expectations you have in your marriage, and then write them down. Now, carefully go over your list. Beside each expectation place an "S" (for shared) if you have shared that one with your spouse and a "U" (unshared) if you have not. Then put a star by each expectation that is realistic and cross off each one that is unrealistic. That last step may be difficult for you. Your pen may run out of ink or your pencil lead may break or your computer may lock up.

Try this: Take each of those expectations before God in prayer. Ask Him to help you with your list. Now what does your list look like? Take your refined list, sit down with your spouse, and go over it with him or her. This is a tough process, but one that will do amazing things for your marriage. Honest evaluations of your expectations can stop the insanity.

Hidden Insanities

The truth is, unrealistic expectations—left unchecked—often turn into insanities. And of course, these "insanities" can sometimes be difficult to see. They may be evident to others, but we are oblivious.

Look at this scenario. Michael grew up in a Christian home. His parents were married in their late twenties, and Michael was born a couple of years later. Michael was the oldest of three children, and his mother stayed at home with them. At about ten years of age, Michael noticed some changes in his mother. In the afternoon when he came home from school she was happy, but as the evening wore on she became agitated and easily angered. There were times she even threw pans across the kitchen and slammed the pantry door.

Michael's dad worked hard and usually late in the evening. He was seldom home before seven. By that time of the day, his mother was more in control, but Michael confided in his dad about his mom's "crazy times." Things did not change much over the next few years. Michael learned to cope with it and thought all moms had these crazy times. Besides, his mom was a Christian, and they went to church every week.

Once Michael began to drive, he stayed away from home in the evening until his dad got home. He had a part-time job and studied at his girlfriend's house. His parents bought it. Michael knew things were not quite right, but it was his "normal," and he learned to adapt.

What Michael did not know as a child was that his mother was addicted to pain medications. Her behaviors were not normal. In fact, they were far from normal, but nobody ever told Michael.

Think with me a minute. What are some of the insanities that Michael could drag into marriage and never see as insanities? Remember, that was his normal, and he believed that there was nothing unusual in his family of origin.

Could Michael fall in love with and marry someone with an addictive personality? Could Michael have an addictive personality? What are some of the things Michael saw as normal that were really unhealthy? How does Michael see his role as a husband and a father? Will he be as absent as his own father was? There are lots of ways this could play out in marriage, and most of them are not good. If things are to be different for Michael, he will need to identify the insanities and begin to deal with them.

Insanities That Haunt from the Past

Jennifer was a victim. In counseling, I see a number of people who put themselves in the victim role, and I see others who are true victims. Jennifer was a true victim. She brought me a picture taken of her on her seventh birthday. She was a beautiful little girl. Her eyes sparkled in the picture, and she had a smile that covered her face. Then Jennifer showed me a picture of her taken on her ninth birthday. As they grow, kids can change a lot, but this change was drastic. Gone was the sparkle in the eyes and the big smile. I was looking at a picture of a nine-year-old girl with sad eyes and an empty look.

Shortly after Jennifer's seventh birthday she was sexually abused by a teen neighbor, and the abuse continued for over two years. She never told anyone because the boy said if she told he would kill her dog, so she stayed silent. Jennifer was the middle child in the family, and it was a busy family. Her parents would ask her what was wrong and then not listen to her answer. Jennifer was an overachiever who dove headfirst into her schoolwork. She made all A's and made the honor roll, and her parents bragged on her often. She learned to stuff down the feelings the abuse caused in her. She ignored them, and when the neighbor boy's family moved away shortly after her ninth birthday, she relaxed. It was over, but she still never told anyone.

Slowly the smile returned but not the sparkle. She had lots of friends, and the boys all thought she was cute even though she wanted nothing to do with them. She had a few dates in high school, but with "good guy" friends she trusted. Mainly she stayed in groups surrounded by her close girlfriends. Jennifer graduated valedictorian of her class and scored high on her college entrance exams. She chose a university close to her house and decided to live at home. That was safe.

During her senior year, Jennifer met David. David was a nice guy. He was a Christian and did Bible study with her and prayed with her. They talked a lot and shared hopes and dreams and values. David was a virgin and was committed to purity till marriage. The night David shared that commitment with Jennifer, she went home, got sick, and cried till she finally fell asleep. The next morning she called me. It was one of those tough calls. I knew this woman was hurting, but I could barely understand what she was saying. Finally, I asked her to come to my office, and there she began to unload her story for the first time ever.

Many of you who are reading this identify with Jennifer at some level. Sexual abuse is way too common in our society. It is devastating and wrong and does great harm to the victim. Jennifer took a first step that literally changed her life. The story she had hidden for so long was now in the light. I will not lie to you. Jennifer's healing process was difficult and took a long time, but today she is a different woman. God has healed her pain and shame, and she lives a life filled with hope. If you saw her picture today, you would see one similar to that seven-year-old little girl on her birthday. The smile and the sparkle are back, and David waited for her.

What if Jennifer never made that first step to get help? Maybe she would have sucked it up and let David believe she was a virgin. Maybe they would date and marry. Or maybe she would continue to see herself as "damaged goods" and never date again.

Let me stop here for just a moment. Please hear this. No matter who you are or what you have done or what has been done to you, *you are not damaged goods.* Period. No one has the right to define you but God, and He says you are fearfully and wonderfully made and through your faith in Christ you are made perfect in His sight. Please never lose sight of this truth.

Maybe Jennifer would marry but never be able to enjoy the sexual relationship in marriage the way God intended. All of these maybes are insanities. They do not address or solve the problem. They perpetu-

> **No matter who you are or what you have done or what has been done to you, *you are not damaged goods.* No one has the right to define you but God.**

ate the false belief that things cannot be different. If this hits close to home for you, promise me one thing. Tomorrow you will call someone and take the first step toward getting help. If you do not, you continue to give power to your abuser. Don't do that. Stop the insanity and embrace the transforming power that God can give you. He has more for you than you could ever imagine.

Facing Your Insanities Together

Insanities come in all kinds of packages. Some are very volatile, while others are not. The choice of where a couple chooses to attend church can cause friction. One of my cases held the possibility of insanity in this realm, but it took a change in life circumstances to bring it to light.

Brian and Laura had been married five years when I first met them in my office. They were a striking couple, and they sat down close to each other on the couch. That kind of body language is usually a good sign in my office, since troubled couples often sit as far from each other as possible.

Brian and Laura communicated their history to me. After meeting at work, they dated about a year and a half and then married. For six days each week their marriage was close to perfect, but when Sunday came, things were far from perfect.

Brian had grown up in an Episcopal church while Laura had grown up as a Baptist. They felt that their beliefs were not that far apart, but they had never been able to resolve which church to attend together. They gave me some history. They started out in their marriage trying to compromise. They attended the church of Brian's choice one Sunday and the church of Laura's choice the next Sunday. That worked pretty well for a year or so.

Brian was content, but Laura wanted more. She wanted to feel more connected to a church and did not think they could do that by bouncing back and forth each week. Laura was shocked when Brian agreed, but she was not excited about his solution: Laura could go to her church, and he would go to his. That way they could both get more involved in the church each wanted to attend. Laura reluctantly agreed.

So for the next two years they followed Brian's plan. Surprisingly, Laura got somewhat used to the idea. If there was a big event at either church, they would attend together. They shared sermon notes with each other, and Brian felt they had the best of both worlds.

What was never really resolved had seemed to work for the two of them. But it was not going to work as their family grew. Laura was pregnant, and a lot of questions began to run through her mind. One of them centered on where the family would attend church. Finally, after much thought and prayer, she brought up the subject to Brian. It was a subject that had never crossed Brian's mind, and he did not see it being an issue.

Then the problem began. Laura was adamant. They had to attend church together as a family. Brian agreed in theory but was still not willing to budge. The next few weeks were tense, to say the least. Conversations were terse and sparse. Finally they agreed to counseling but were not hopeful that a resolution could be found.

My belief is that a marriage has to be centered on God. Doesn't it just make sense that the author of marriage Himself probably has the best plan for a marriage? I think there is great value in a husband and a wife attending the same church together on a regular basis since one of the ways He has provided for us to grow closer to Him and to others is the church. It is not a cure-all for marriage, but it sure helps a lot.

I have counseled couples who do not go to church, couples who one goes and the other does not, couples who go to separate churches, and couples who worship together Sunday after Sunday in the same church. In my unscientific survey, the couples who worship together weekly in the same church have better marriages than any other arrangement.

As I sat with Brian and Laura, I asked them many questions about what each liked about the church they attended and what they did not like about the other's church. This was more complicated than I thought it would be, because they both had many items for the list. I then asked them to name some churches their friends attended that they felt were good churches.

Then came the challenge. I asked them if they would trust me in an experiment. They looked at me and then each other and then laughed and said okay. I gave them a list of three churches different from the ones they had been attending and told them that I felt each of the churches met many of the things on their lists they liked and almost none of the things they did not like. They also had friends at each of the churches.

I asked them to visit each of the churches three times over the next nine Sundays. At the end of the nine weeks, they were to choose one church and begin going there. This would be their new church home.

Then a funny thing happened. They again looked at each other, nodded, and said okay. Honestly, I had never tried that process before, but I am big on problem solving, and I believe God always has an answer for us.

The week before the baby was born Brian and Laura came back to see me. They had a new church home and they loved it. They decided to visit each church once. After round one and much prayer TOGETHER, they knew without a doubt where they were to go. God made it perfectly clear to both of them.

I was pretty sure that would happen. God wants us in church, He wants us united, and He is not a God of confusion. He was not going to lead Brian one way and Laura another. The insanity stopped. Brian, Laura, and God worked together and found a solution that brought healing to their marriage.

Your Turn

Every couple has their insanities. As you read about Richard and Lisa, you may have thought that no one makes that many mistakes over and over. I promise you that they do. If over half of first marriages end in divorce, do you think the stat for second marriages is better? No. It is worse. I have counseled people on their sixth marriage. If we do not stop the insanity, we will repeat the same pattern over and over and over. Richard and Lisa did not initially come to counseling to get help; they had already given up. But after soul searching, they decided to give it one more try.

When Nancy and I married young, we had no idea what marriage was really about. We made a lot of mistakes. We fought bad, unfair fights. We threatened divorce and were a step away from following through after year seven. We had insanities coming out of our ears, but through all our craziness, we did one thing right. One thing that made all the difference in the world: We prayed together. We got honest with both God and each other about our insanities, and He honored that in a powerful way. He healed our insanities and lifted us off the roller coaster of our craziness.

Many of you come from families of origin where there has been a lot of dysfunction like Michael experienced. Your normal was not normal, but you did not know it. The source may have been one or both of your parents or a sibling. The list of dysfunctions seems to be endless. However, we have a choice. We can continue the pattern or break it. Michael, for example, could just stay away from home as a teen, but if he wanted a healthy marriage as an adult, he had to address the insanities he saw in the home he grew up in. There would be a lot of steps for him. Yet, God had a better life for him, without the insanities.

And finally, if you are truly a victim, that does not mean you are doomed to being stuck your whole life in that role. But staying stuck is insanity. Trust me in this. There are answers and healing where you never thought there could be. Where you feel unlovable, there is eternal love and acceptance. Where you feel broken, there can be wholeness. Jennifer took that first step and today is a different person. It is your choice, and only you can take step one, but I promise that if you take that step you will never regret it. Take it today and never look back.

Don't stop short with a Band-Aid solution like Brian and Laura did with going to different churches. Like a lot of us, they settled for a temporary fix. The insanity seemed to stop, but it was only on a short hiatus. Don't settle. Work it out. Get help. Talk to someone. It is insane not to. Follow it through to a solution as they finally did.

Look at some questions and thoughts with me:

- Where is your marriage today?
- If you rated it on a one-to-ten scale with ten being the best, where would it fall?
- How would that compare to a year ago or five years ago?
- Where do you want it to be this time next year?

One of the things that Nancy and I fell into was identifying problems, talking about how we wanted things to be different, and then doing nothing. Time would pass, and things seemed better, and then the unaddressed insanities would surface again. Each time they surfaced, they stayed longer and got uglier, a marriage-killing cycle.

There are seven secrets to an Awesome Marriage in this book. Each one is unique and stands on its own, but together, they have the power to transform your relationship as you know it. You cannot go to secret two until you deal with secret one.

If you are or ever have been involved in any type of twelve-step program, you understand the process. Step one is always admitting you have a problem, whether it is alcohol, drugs, sex, gambling, or whatever. Until the person admits things are out of control and he cannot do anything about it, healing never takes place.

Welcome to step one of having an awesome marriage. This step is true whatever your status. Whether you are married, divorced, single, or something else, you have a problem. You have your own insanities, and without intervention, you will bring them into your relationships and never be able to live out God's plan for your marriage. Wherever you are, acknowledge that you have a problem. And welcome again to step one of having an awesome marriage.

The first step is always the most difficult, but nothing will ever change until you take it.

Some of you are thinking that I am not talking to you, but here's the simple truth: I am talking to me and you and everyone else. We cannot live in this world today and not have a few insanities. Sure, some are worse than others, but we all have them.

Take this challenge:

Set aside some time alone. Bring a notebook, a pen, and your Bible. Make sure it is quiet and there are no distractions. (Turn off the TV.) Ask God to guide you and to show you the insanities in your life. Then write. Write whatever comes to your mind. If God prompts you to open the Bible and read, do it. Then ask God to show you how those insanities are affecting you and your relationships.

If you are married, share what you learned with each other, and then commit to taking whatever steps are necessary to rid your life and your marriage of those insanities. This can be a turning point in your marriage. This can stop the insanity and give you hope that you never had before.

The first step is always the most difficult, but nothing will ever change until you take it. Whatever is standing in your way is not worth it. Stopping the insanity is the first secret, and today is the time to embrace it.

START

The Practice of Putting God First, Spouse Second

Life was pretty good for me growing up—until I hit puberty, that is. My dad's parents lived on a small farm, and it was my favorite place in the world. This was the place where I spent most of my summer days each year. School and books and having to study were a million miles away. I had everything I needed. There was a horse to ride, pigs to feed, eggs to gather, and crops to reap.

As much as I loved the days, the nights were really special. My granddad (Pop) and I would lie side by side in our two hammocks gazing at the stars. It was magical. The sky was so dark and the stars were so bright. I knew about God because as far back as I could remember, our family always went to church, but my first real awareness of the awesomeness of God came on those summer nights. I couldn't get my mind completely around it, but I knew this God was really big, and somehow I began to see that He cared about me.

Pop was a big part of that process as he taught me about unconditional love. No matter what I did, he loved me, and it made me want to return his love and do the things he wanted me to do. This amazing relationship had a huge impact on my life.

Pop was one of those Christians who never went around telling people that he was a Christian. He didn't have to. It was written all over him in the way he lived his life and how he treated people. Sure, if he had the chance, he would tell people about Jesus, but most of the time he just lived like he thought Jesus wanted him to live. At an early age, I decided that was how I wanted to live, too.

Maybe one of my greatest attractions to the farm was the fact that it was pretty easy to do what I thought God wanted me to do when I was there. There was not a teacher making me do things or kids bugging me or parents making me eat things that were good for me. My days and nights were filled with doing all the things that I wanted to do. I remember thinking as I was getting older that I wanted time to stand still. Kids on my block at home were growing up, and I did not like what I saw. If I could just stay eleven and be on the farm forever, I didn't think life could get any better.

I used to think about Adam—the first guy in the Bible. God put him in this perfect garden and loved him unconditionally. I liked the story and thought Adam and I had some things in common. He had the garden and I had the farm. Things were good at the farm for me, and things were good in the garden for him. We both had someone to love us unconditionally. I wondered if Adam ever wanted things to just stand still like I did. Yet I found that there was one big fallacy about wanting things to stand still. They won't and they don't. I grew up, and Adam ate the apple.

The summer I turned twelve found me spending only half of my days on the farm. I had friends that wanted me to go to the lake with them, and there was this new girl that moved in down the street from my house. I still loved the farm, but I was beginning to love my other life, too. By my thirteenth summer, the farm was relegated to just a couple of weekend trips. I was growing up and my interests were changing; the following God thing was getting a whole lot tougher, too.

Things also changed for Adam. This woman, Eve, came into his life, and the plan was that they were supposed to bring out the best in each other. God put them together and placed them in this incredible, enjoyable paradise. That plan worked for a while, but then things got really messed up. Eve listened to a lie and ate a piece of fruit that God told them not to eat, and then she gave some to Adam and he ate it too. As they were digesting their fruit, God came into the garden, and Adam realized his time in the garden was over. That fruit thing that seemed like such a good idea at the time was not.

If Adam and Eve could have a do over, do you think they would jump at the opportunity? I know I would. The need for do overs was becoming evident to me as I navigated my way through middle school and high school. Like Adam and Eve, I was slipping away from God. I listened to people I should not have listened to and did things I never should have done. I often found myself in messes just like Adam and Eve's.

Adam and Eve probably thought God had given up on them. They probably wondered if they would ever hear from God again. As I looked at my life, I was not sure what God thought of me, either. I did try to touch base with Him every once in a while, but I usually didn't stay in touch long enough to see if He was there or not. It had been a long time since I lay in a hammock on a dark night looking at the stars.

Have you ever had a time like that in your life? Have you had a time when God seemed so far away that you had no hope of ever reaching Him again? It seems those are the times we see Him show up. Just when we think He is gone, He isn't. Just when we think He has given up on us, we realize that He hasn't. This God of creation is a God of love.

It is often when our nights are the darkest that He shines the brightest. Adam and Eve were on the outside of the garden. It seemed that all was lost, and then He showed up again. It was not paradise, but life went on and God was with them. They had a baby boy and then they had another. They tended the land they now lived in, and it prospered.

One generation led to another, and lots of baby boys were

born all the way down to this baby boy named Jesus. God reached out and fixed things. He was there for Adam and Eve, and He is there for you and me. No matter how far we have strayed, He has given us a way back to Him. Jesus' family tree goes all the way back to Adam and all the way forward to you and to me. Amazing, isn't it?

Think about this. God created everything—including us. He also created marriage. Now this is the cool part. Just as God has a perfect plan for your life starting with the day you were conceived, He also has a perfect plan for your marriage—starting at the altar.

I take my car to the dealership when it needs service, because the dealer knows my car. It is one of theirs. They know what makes it run the best, and they understand what it needs when it is not working well. You can get marriage advice from myriad sources, but why go to sources when you can go to the Source? Just like my dealer knows my car, God knows marriage. He knows it inside out and upside down. He even has this unique plan for you because each marriage is unique. He knows exactly what you need and exactly what your spouse needs and exactly what your marriage needs.

Just when we think He has given up on us, we realize that He hasn't. This God of creation is a God of love.

That is more than awesome. It borders on miraculous! So you have a choice. You can do things your own way and ignore God, or you can seek Him and His plan for your life and your marriage. The choice is yours. We can learn from the mistakes Adam and Eve made, or we can repeat them over and again. Choose you or choose God. Over the years of my life I haven't always chosen to put God first, but today I do. I choose God.

> ### *What will you choose?*
>
> If you choose God, do you really have anything to lose? If I am wrong, you have wasted a few days that you probably would have wasted anyway, but if I am right, you can have a life and a marriage that are better than anything you could imagine. It's your turn at the plate. It's your choice. What will you choose? It is time to start!

Putting God First Through Prayer

On our wedding night, Nancy and I knelt by the side of the bed in our bridal suite and prayed. We didn't know it then, but that night we began to lay a foundation of regular prayer together that has made an indescribable difference in our marriage. Prayer together has literally been the glue that kept us together through storm after storm.

I wish I could tell you that I planned that first prayer, but I did not. The idea to pray on our first night as husband and wife was Nancy's. On the outside, I was praying, but on the inside I was saying, I can't wait to get this over with and get on with our wedding night together. I was not there spiritually, but do you know what I later realized? God was, and He honored my feeble attempt to connect with Him.

Nancy had taken much more time to think through this marriage thing than I had. A wise woman had advised her of the importance of a husband and a wife praying together in marriage. Nancy took her seriously, and over the years of our marriage we have knelt by the bed together almost every evening in prayer.

Looking back, I have learned a lot about a husband and a wife praying regularly together. There is something about the regularity. Some nights I feel connected to God and Nancy, and some nights I feel distant. Some nights I cannot wait to pray with her, and others

I could not care less. If I went with my feelings, our nights of prayer in marriage would be closer to 25 percent rather than 95 percent.

It is not about whether I feel like it or not. Rather, it is about consistently coming before God together and laying our life together before Him. I strongly believe there is power in consistency. Not that God has a scoreboard in the sky that records prayers as points, but rather that our kneeling together night after night gave us the opportunity to lay every care, concern, joy, and sorrow before the Lord.

We have seen Him show up with answers to prayer more times than either of us can count. Some were dramatic. Some were simple. Some were "no," but He always was there. We felt like a team—me, Nancy, and God. Together we have found that we are unbeatable.

But sometimes praying together was far more than a routine. Sometimes, it was a lifeline—like after our son was born. We had been married five and a half years and had waited with great expectation for that moment. Things seemed good in our marriage—we were now a family.

Yet the next year was not what I wanted or expected it to be. Nancy and I grew apart. We went through the normal pattern that often happens when a baby comes. I felt a little left out. Many evenings we were both tired and often irritable, and in looking back, there were some issues we had avoided dealing with that were now coming to the surface. One of these was taking each other for granted. So we fought more and did not fight well.

The closeness that we both cherished became distant and short-lived. We talked about it a lot, but the talks were doing more harm than good. I would get angry, and she knew I was not hearing what she was saying. I never thought we would part, but one night after a difficult argument Nancy said she was thinking that we might need to separate or divorce. She told me she was confused and did not think she really wanted a divorce, but she was just not happy. I felt like the wind had been knocked out of me. I hurt in a way that I had never hurt before.

I didn't know what to do. I didn't want to lose her and our family that we waited so long to have. So I prayed and Nancy prayed. We prayed together and we prayed individually. We asked God for help, to do for us what we could not do for ourselves. I wondered what God would do. Would He act at all? I had never really doubted in the past, but suddenly, I was not sure.

Nancy has always found good women to be mentors in her life. At this time of crisis in our marriage, she sought the counsel of an older woman in our church. Nancy went to the lady with a story of her "friend" who was struggling in her marriage.

The story Nancy unfolded was ours, packaged as someone else's. But this wise woman wasn't fooled, as she told Nancy years later. Her counsel to Nancy was this, "Tell your friend to not give up. Tell her not to leave her marriage based on her feelings because they will change from time to time. Marriage is a commitment for a lifetime. Tell her to love her husband and to put God first." Nancy and her "friend" said thanks, and she followed the advice of this woman God had placed in her life.

You may be in the same place today that Nancy was years ago. You started your marriage with hopes and dreams that now seem shattered. Deep inside you hate the thought of divorce and the pain it brings, but you also know that you cannot go on living in your marriage unless something changes. This is where we found ourselves. As I look back over the years of our marriage, most of the memories are very good, but this time in our lives still has a dark black cloud over it. The knot in my stomach was there all the time, and even as I write this I can feel the knot beginning again.

There were three things that I think made the difference for us. First, Nancy sought out a wise mentor who was a very strong Christian woman. Second, in the midst of all the pain, I had to let her go if she needed to go. I could not have her stay because I manipulated her. She had to stay because she made the decision to stay. Third, we both sought God and literally let Him guide us step by step through this darkness. It was not a quick fix, but over time our marriage began to grow again, and together we buried the divorce word forever.

Over the years there have been many other storms in our lives. Some came because we were screwing up our marriage, and some came from the outside. Each of these storms rocked our boat, but we never capsized. We learned to ride them out and also learned that on the other side were always calm waters again. The fact that we were consistently praying during both the good and bad times made a difference. Even when we did not feel like praying, we did. There was something about the regularity that made a huge difference. It taught us to put God first. It taught us that He always had an answer for every problem. It gave us hope when the world told us there was none. If we had not made prayer a consistent part of our life together, the odds of us making it would not have been good.

Praying together every night encouraged us to resolve issues or at least call a truce before prayer time. So what about you? How often do you and your spouse pray together? Probably not often. One survey says that less than 8 percent of Christian couples pray regularly together.[1] Isn't that amazing? I mean, as Christians, we know better. There is power in prayer. We have the ear of the Creator of the universe, and we fail to whisper into it.

If as a couple you are praying, don't stop. Do not let anything get in the way of this routine. But if you as a couple are not praying together, do not let anything get in the way of starting this vital practice.

The God Who Changes Hearts

When couples come to see me for marriage counseling, they usually have an agenda. They tell me the problem and they want me to fix it. Guess what? It does not work that way. Helping a couple improve their marriage involves a process. I help them

---

1. Dennis Rainey, "Prayer: The Secret to a Lasting Marriage," FamilyLife. com, 2001, http://www.christianity.com/christian-life/marriage-and-family/ prayer-the-secret-to-a-lasting-marriage-11545181.html.

identify the real problem. Together we explore solutions and find one that seems to fit. Next they try it out, and then we evaluate together. That process usually works, but if I want to work myself out of a job with them (which is my goal with every couple), there is much more that needs to be done.

Most of us can make changes to make things better at least for the short term. But change for the long term is different. That involves a heart change, and who better to change a heart but God?

Mark and Patricia made an attractive couple. They had been married seven years and had two children. Both of them worked but had the same weekend days off. Money was tight, but they had no debt. I was their fourth counselor. I asked them about their previous counseling experiences—what they liked and didn't like. For the most part, they liked the other counselors and felt they had been helpful.

I asked them why they came to me instead of going back to one of the other counselors. Their answer was not what I expected. Even though each counselor had helped them through

Change for the long term is different. That involves a heart change, and who better to change a heart but God?

the current problem that they were facing, they did not seem to be breaking the patterns that caused the problems in their marriage. They felt they were on a cycle of having a problem, solving the problem, having a time of peace, and having a problem again. "Isn't there something we can do to break this cycle?"

I answered them carefully. My answer was yes. Yes, there was something they could do. They could let God change their hearts. That statement always gets me curious looks even though it is usually not the first time someone has heard that idea. If they are Christians and have been in church for any length of time at all, they had to have come across that concept. It sounds good. It certainly sounds "spiritual." The problem is that most of us have no idea how to get there, and we all have barriers that stand in our way.

> ### *Action Steps*
>
> Letting God change our hearts is a simple three-step process. It is following through and keeping the change that often presents the challenge.
>
> - Step one is simply admitting that we have been selfish and have put our wants and desires above those of God, stopping the insanity.
> - Step two is making the commitment to put God first in everything and seeking His help in doing this.
> - Step three is keeping God first every day for the rest of our lives.

Have I lost you? Are you saying, "I thought this was a marriage book, not a book about God"? My premise is this: If God created us and marriage, who would know better how to make it work?

The Cost of Choosing the Wrong Thing First

When I have an issue with my car, what do I do? I take it to the dealership that has trained repairmen who know how to solve the problem and make it run again. If the air-conditioning in my home goes out, I call the person who installed the system to come and see what is wrong. He can diagnose the problem and give me a solution. If there is a problem in my marriage, where do I go? The logical answer would be to the One who created it, but that is often the last place we go. We try to solve it our way, and that just does not work—at least not in the long term. The following scenarios demonstrate some of the many ways people will try to cope with failing marriages in their own ways. Do any of these tactics look familiar to you?

Steven was sick of the fighting. His wife was so critical of him. Day after day she nagged and told him all the things he should be doing that he was not and all the things he should not be doing that he was. The last time she affirmed or encouraged him was so long ago he could not remember it.

But Betty in the office down the hall listened to him. She seemed to admire Steven and praised him for his accomplishments at work. He liked running into her at work and was becoming more and more familiar with her schedule so he could "bump" into her several times each day. One Thursday they ended up in front of the elevator together at lunch time. On the ride down, Steven asked her to eat with him, and she did. They began to have lunch together most days. Betty was such a good listener. She understood him in a way he did not think his wife ever had.

With the new project in the office, Steven and Betty found themselves working together late a couple of times a week. Dinner together seemed the thing to do. Then there was the dinner at the new restaurant in the hotel across the street. A nice dinner. Some intimate conversation and a few drinks. Steven went to the front desk, rented a room, and he and Betty took the next step.

In another situation, there was Sharon, who loved her husband. He was good to her, and there was nothing she wanted that he did not provide. Well, almost nothing. He was gone a lot. He worked hard, and they both had agreed on the lifestyle they were living. Sharon just did not realize the price she would pay for it. He left early in the morning and came home late at night. They usually ate dinner together, but he was so tired that there was little conversation. He saw the weekends as his time to get away, and he played golf both days. Sometimes, if it was raining or the weather was bad, they went to church; but that was not often. They usually went out for a nice dinner on Saturday night and had sex when they got home. He seemed happy with their life, but Sharon was not happy at all.

Sharon's mother was an alcoholic. Sharon could never understand why her mother drank, but now the pieces began to fit together. It was a way to escape. Sharon made a trip to the liquor store. She bought twelve bottles of wine because it was a better deal, and she returned home and uncorked a bottle. Having a glass in the afternoon to take her mind off things seemed like such a good idea, and she could control it. One glass a day. That one-glass-a-day thing lasted a week and then went to two a day and then a bottle a day. The people at the liquor store soon knew her name and they were so nice to her. They were her new friends. Life was better.

———

Just starting off in life, William was determined to have a marriage different from his parents'. They stayed together, but they were like two strangers living under the same roof. Not William. Not his marriage. His would be different, and it was for the first few years. He and his wife were deeply in love and spent every minute together that they could. His job was demanding, but he was content with the status quo and did not need to be on the fast track. His marriage was more important. William was sure he was breaking the cycle. He loved it being just the two of them, but they had agreed on having a family, and it was time to start.

The next four years brought three pregnancies and three baby girls. Each was special and beautiful, and William was a proud father. The change was gradual, but his wife's attention shifted from William to the girls. She was a great mom, but he felt he was losing his wife. If he came home early from work, she was occupied with the children. If he wanted to make love, she was exhausted.

William became lonely and thought his marriage was beginning to mirror that of his parents. Something had to change, and he was convinced he was the one who needed to figure things out. He made an appointment with his boss and bluntly asked him what it would take for William to become a partner in the firm.

His boss was elated and told William he knew the day would come when he would want to realize his full potential. They set out a three-year plan, which William was determined to accomplish in eighteen months. William went home and shared the news with his wife. She congratulated him and went in the kitchen to prepare the girls' dinner. William went to his home office and sat down in front of his computer.

Now there is nothing wrong with a husband seeking to better himself in his job or career, but William's decision was colored by his loneliness and frustration with his marriage. Basically William was saying, "If I cannot get my needs met in my marriage, I will get them met in my career." William turned his back on his marriage and put everything into his career. As William succeeded at work, his marriage continued to fail.

I have often thought about marriage as a superhighway. We have a starting point and an ending point. The starting point is our wedding day, and the ending point comes way down the highway fifty years or so later. The goal is not just to finish but to finish well. The goal is to have and to build an awesome marriage. On this highway there are exits. Actually, there are lots of exits. The couples who finish well stay on the highway and avoid the exits. There are times they might consider exiting. The road gets rough or there are hazards. Some couples even put on their blinker as a first step to exiting but stay the course and pass the exit by.

Steven found Betty and took an exit. Sharon began drinking and that became her exit. William made partner in eighteen months and never realized he took an exit. There are all kinds of exits. Some are destructive like alcohol and drug abuse. Others are not destructive in themselves but ultimately destroy a marriage. Which gets us back to God. What if Steven had pursued God instead of Betty? What if Sharon pursued God instead of alcohol? What if William pursued God before getting on the fast track?

Would God have been there for them? Would they have been able to stay on the marriage highway? I believe the answer is yes, but in our culture today most people never give God the chance.

What about you? Are you thinking about an exit? Maybe your blinker is on or you have already taken an exit. Wherever you are, it is not too late. God is right where He always has been and is ready to jump right into the middle of your life. All you need to do is invite Him in.

Taking Spiritual Responsibility in Your Marriage

Paul and Sarah were young and newly married. We began their premarital counseling a couple of months before the wedding. I told them that if we did not get everything covered before their wedding day, we would pick back up when they returned from their honeymoon. Today was pickup day. They were an amazing couple, and I looked forward to spending time with them. They were both church kids, and their faith had been a part of their lives as long as they could remember. They got the concept of putting God first and not letting anything take second place other than each other. They were way ahead of the game.

With all I have learned about people over the years, I still amaze myself at some of the assumptions I make. Because I knew Paul's and Sarah's backgrounds and quite a bit about each of their families, I just skimmed over much of the teaching I do about pursuing God. After all, they were both Christians and had been pursuing God individually for a long time. Pursuing Him together should have been easy. As I finished telling them how important it was for couples to pray together every day, Paul gave me a blank stare. Then he said, "How do we do that?"

So much for my assumption.

After talking with literally hundreds of husbands, I know that one of the most difficult tasks men face is being the spiritual leader of their homes. The reasons why usually fall into one of three areas. First, most men felt inadequate. Second, few had ever had spiritual leadership modeled for them. Third, many felt that their wives were far superior to them in spiritual matters.

As we married, I claimed all three. So on that first night of our marriage as we knelt together by the side of the bed to pray, Nancy looked at me and said, "Would you like to start?" Inside I was screaming no, and I guess my face was conveying the same message. I had never prayed out loud before anyone. Then as I mentally shuffled through my repertoire of prayers (which did not take long), I came up empty. Nancy suggested that we say the Lord's Prayer together. I had forgotten about that one, but I did know it and was totally on board. So that is what we did. We held hands, bowed our heads, closed our eyes, and said the Lord's Prayer. We soon added silent prayer to our routine. Each of us would share things we wanted to pray for and about, and then both of us would pray silently.

> **There is not a right way to pray. God longs to spend time with us. He is more about us coming to Him than about the way we do it.**

If you decide to pursue God together through prayer (and I am praying that you will), where would you start? You may have a good idea. Some of you may have been praying together already, but if you are new at this, let me give you some ideas.

It is important to remember that there is not a right way to pray. I believe God longs to spend time with us. He is more about us coming to Him than about the way we do it. Remember Adam and Eve? The Bible tells us that God would come every day to the garden to spend time with them. There is your picture. That is what God wants with you, and because Jesus has provided a way for us to be reconciled to God, that relationship is there for the taking. Your step one is making the commitment to pray together.

Let me challenge you to commit to pray together every day for the next thirty days. Here are some ideas for you. They are in no particular order. Find one you are both comfortable with, and you are off and running. Here we go!

First, Three Cautions:
- It does not matter how long you pray. Start with a minute and see what happens.
- It does not matter if you pray silently or out loud. God has incredible hearing.
- It does not matter if you are kneeling, standing, sitting, or lying in bed. Just pray.

Ideas:
- Talk together about things you want to pray about. Then pray.
- Hold hands and pray silently together. Squeeze the hand of your spouse when you are done.
- Pray the Lord's Prayer together (Matthew 6:9–13). This is the prayer Jesus taught us. It's a good place to start.
- Pick a topic and pray about it. You can pray for your marriage, your kids, the world, or each other.
- Find a Bible verse that fits your current situation in life, and pray it together.

When Nancy and I began praying together, on our wedding night and beyond, we prayed silently and then repeated the Lord's Prayer together. It worked for me. I could do this prayer. It kept me at a level of praying with Nancy that I was comfortable with, and I truly believe that from the beginning, God honored our faithfulness to pray. Often, it united us and put us on the same page. Praying together also softened our hearts toward each other in times of stress and strife. It was just really difficult for me to stay mad at someone I was praying with. The two, for me, did not work well together.

Our next step was to share with each other our concerns and things we wanted to take before God together in prayer. The items on our list changed from day to day, week to week, and year to year. We silently prayed for our marriage, other people's marriages, for our families, for our children, for wisdom as parents, for our pastor, for our church, for the needy, and for the hungry. You get the idea. Whatever was on our hearts we shared with each other and then silently prayed together before God. It was amazing. He heard us, and He answered so many of our prayers. We grew closer to Him and closer to each other.

Then one day Nancy did something she had never done in front of me before. She did not pray silently. She prayed out loud. She took a step I had been reluctant to take. I love my comfort zones, and I was in one with our silent prayer life. Now my wife rocked my boat. I knew that just because she prayed out loud did not mean I had to do the same. Yet there was something special about hearing her take our common concerns before God. God was growing us in our spiritual life together with Him. It did not happen the next night or the one after that, but before too long I was also praying out loud.

Other couples have shared their ideas about praying with me. Some write out prayers and then share them with each other. Some pray specific Bible verses that are applicable to their circumstances. Some couples never pray out loud. In some marriages, only one prays out loud. The bottom line is this: do not get caught up in the details—just pray.

A few years ago as the Christmas holidays were ending, Nancy and I were talking about some things that we were both concerned about. They were some of those things that you worry about but have no control over. We had three that we could not shake. We made an agreement that beginning the first of the new year we would pray together for God to act in those three circumstances. We knew that if something happened or changed in any one of the three things that it would totally be a God deal.

On January first, we began. We were faithful with this and hardly missed a day. Hold on to your seat. By August of that year, every one of these three prayers was completely answered. In our minds, it was God working three miracles. We prayed, and He did the work.

Now this has not always been our experience. Sometimes we pray, and the answer seems to be no, or later, or wait (which is really hard for me). But I know God always hears our prayers, and I know He always does what is best for us, and I know that He is always good. I can live with that. In fact, I can rejoice in that.

Worship and Serving Together

I heard Tommy Nelson of Denton Bible Church say to a group of singles one time that they should run as hard as they could pursuing God and then look over and see who was running with them. That might be the right person to ask to run with you. I like that. It is great advice for singles, but how about adapting it for marriage? If I am running as fast as I can for God and Nancy is doing the same, don't we have a pretty good chance of keeping Him first in our lives and in our marriage? Don't you think we can run that pursuit together? I do, and I know that is what God wants. Let's look at a few other ways to pursue God together.

Worship is a moving experience for many of us. Sometimes it is a time-out from the world. We can focus on God and listen to Him. For me, a worship service has become both a personal and a shared experience. There are times God speaks to me through music, the Bible, and the message.

I love leaving a service after having an encounter with God. When Nancy is by my side singing the same songs, reading the same Scriptures, and hearing the same message, the spiritual oneness that occurs is priceless. After the service, we can share with each other what we learned and what we thought God was saying to us. Sometimes what we take away is similar, and sometimes it is different; but we see God at work within us and our marriage. Worshipping with your spouse is another way to pursue God together.

We were married only a couple of years the first time Nancy

and I served together. It was Christmastime, and the little church we were attending made a commitment to provide food, clothing, and gifts for a group of less fortunate families. Nancy picked up our list at the church office. We had a single mom with three kids all under ten years of age. The mother listed the kids' clothes sizes and some ideas of what they needed.

Early on a Saturday morning, we went shopping, and we had a ball. We bought the necessities, and then we (really I) went crazy on the toys. Our car was packed and we were so excited. It was the first time we stopped to consider how blessed we were and what a joy it was to share our blessings with others, and we were doing it together.

God taught us a lot through that experience. It put a different spin on Christmas. It became all about Him instead of all about us. Maybe the most important lesson we took away was that the family we helped never knew our names and nobody told us what a great job we did or how they admired us. We simply met the mom, handed all the gifts over to her, and left. It is a tradition we have repeated year after year, and serving others together always brings us closer to God and to each other.

Over the years, we have had lots of great opportunities to serve God as a couple. Twice we were invited to a conference in Amsterdam to help church leaders from third world countries. It was a powerful experience, and God taught us so much during those trips. Every other week Nancy helps serve lunch to a group of homeless people in our city. The few times I have been able to serve there alongside her have been rewarding.

Opportunities are all around you. Help the needy; connect with Habitat for Humanity or another helping agency in your area. Serve in your church, or go on a mission trip together. The list is limited only by your imagination. Serving together is a win-win deal. As a couple you help others, and as a couple you help your marriage. What are you waiting for? Find a project or need and start serving together today.

I was reading about the low rate of divorce among Christian couples who regularly read the Bible together. As I thought it through, it made a lot of sense. The Bible is God's Word, and we know it transforms lives. Why not marriages?

I was sharing the benefits of couples reading the Bible together with Josh. Josh is twenty-six and studying to be a counselor. I have invested time in him for over a year and am excited to see his passion for helping others. Josh's wife, Stacy, teaches first grade at an inner-city school. They are a great couple and work hard at everything they do, including marriage. Josh is bright and is still doing classwork for his master's degree. He is fascinated with statistics, and the statistic about Bible reading helping marriages got his attention. He left my office that day determined to share this news with Stacy and to begin reading the Bible together with her that night.

By the time we met the following week, I had totally forgotten about our Bible-reading talk. Josh sat down, looked at me, and then spoke. "Remember that idea you gave me about reading the Bible with Stacy? How do you do that?" I asked him what happened, and he unpacked the story for me. During dinner Josh shared the idea with Stacy and she agreed they would start that night.

As they sat down, Stacy asked him where they were going to start. Josh had no idea. Stacy suggested they just let their Bible fall open and begin there. She had seen that in some TV show, and it seemed to work well on the show. Josh held up

The main thing is to start and to pursue God together through His written word. It will begin to knit the two of you together with God in a powerful way.

their Bible and let it fall open. There before him was the twenty-sixth chapter of the book of Numbers, and Josh began reading all the names taken in some census after some plague. Certainly there is value in every verse in the Bible, but this was not exactly what Josh had in mind for himself and Stacy.

There are a number of ways to read the Bible together. One of our favorites is to pick from the many plans available on the You Version Bible app.[2]

Certainly, you can do as Josh did and let it fall open and begin reading. I have talked to people who like that idea and know God has spoken to them that way. You can also go together to a Christian bookstore and pick out a Bible study to do together. There are many different kinds, from ones dealing with marriage to almost any topic imaginable.

There are many wonderful reading plans on some of the computer and mobile Bible apps. Some couples choose to read through the Psalms or Proverbs together. This year Nancy and I are doing the same read-through-the-Bible-in-a-year plan. We read it separately, but we are reading the same thing each day and can interact together on what we are reading. The main thing is to start and to pursue God together through His written word. It will begin to knit the two of you together with God in a powerful way.

When the Praying Gets Hard

One of the great mysteries of marriage for me is this: If pursuing God is what God wants us to do and when we pursue Him together our marriages improve, why do we stop pursuing?

Robert and Linda were determined to change the course of their marriage. It was not a bad marriage. They did not fight much, and when they did, they usually resolved the issue. They enjoyed their time together and also found time for their own interests. Attending church was a part of their routine, and they seldom missed. As their pastor completed a series on marriage, they decided to add some of his suggestions to their life together. They would begin with praying together and then look for opportunities to serve together.

Finding a time to pray together was more difficult than they imagined. Robert went to bed before Linda each evening. In the

---

2. https://www.youversion.com.

mornings, Robert was long gone by the time Linda got her day going. For a week they did nothing, and then one evening Robert asked Linda to pray with him right before he went to bed. They prayed together every night for a week, but the time varied, and it was messing with Linda's favorite TV shows. Linda wanted a consistent time to pray, and they agreed on five minutes past nine.

Over the next seven days, they prayed together three times. Two of the nights Robert was already asleep when Linda came into the bedroom at 9:05 p.m. One night Linda was engrossed in a two-hour TV special and forgot all about praying until she came to bed late. The other night they both forgot. Praying together seemed like a good idea, and they even encouraged their friends to try it. But their schedules weren't working, and they would need to get creative before finding a solution.

Some couples have no problem setting a schedule and keeping it. Jessica and Joseph fit in that category. They loved the idea of praying together. In fact, they had prayed together sporadically over the three years of their marriage. Now they would pray every day. Together they made a list of prayer concerns. They decided what they would pray for together and could not wait to see God act.

We all seem to have our own expectations when we bring things before God in prayer. For some, they see God like this big Santa Claus who grants every wish. Others feel unworthy to come before God and have trouble believing God will hear their prayers, let alone answer them. Some of us focus on ourselves when praying, while others have trouble asking for anything.

My belief is that God is a loving father who loves for His children to come to Him in prayer. I believe that God hears every prayer His children pray. I also believe He answers every prayer, even when He says no or is silent. That is where people get hung up. They ask, "Why pray?" if the answer is not going to be a quick yes.

When Jessica and Joseph started to pray together, they expected a quick yes, and it did not come. They continued to pray, and it still did not come. After three weeks their enthusiasm waned, and they just quit trying. They wondered if they had done something wrong, coming up with empty answers.

Nancy and I have missed very few nights praying together. A few times we missed when one of us was sick. Most of the time when one of us was traveling, we managed to pray together over the phone. But there were a few times when we did not pray because we were in an argument. One of the cool things about praying regularly together is the commitment. We are doing this every night no matter what! So there were times when we were in an argument that we honored our commitment to pray. Begrudgingly, I would kneel by Nancy's side and offer her my hand (kind of) and begin to pray. Do you know what would happen by the time we were finished praying? We were not upset anymore.

I think it is almost impossible for a couple to come together in prayer before the God of the universe and walk away angry. It just does not work that way. So back to the few nights we did not pray because we were fighting. Do you know why I did not pray with Nancy? Because I wanted to stay mad; and I knew if we prayed together, my heart would change. Is that sick or what?

Though I don't think I'm the only one. Just ask Melissa and Kevin. They wanted a better marriage and decided to commit to praying together. They decided the when and where and agreed to begin that evening. During dinner, Kevin made a negative comment about the food Melissa prepared as he carried his plate to the trash can to dispose of it. No prayer that night. The next night they ate out, so no food prep comments. On the way home, Melissa asked Kevin to go to her sister's birthday party with her on Saturday afternoon. Kevin made a rude comment about the sister.

They got home, went their separate ways, and no prayer. The next three nights all contained scenarios that ended in a fight, and they eluded prayer time together. As they sat side by side in church on Sunday, Melissa and Kevin realized that they fought a lot, and their fights were keeping them from pursuing God together in prayer. They both hated the situation they were in and wished things were different, but they were not. They left church and began fighting before they left the church parking lot.

Your Turn

The previous stories are just a few of many. Pursuing God together in marriage takes time, persistence, and commitment. There will be days you just don't feel like it and days you just get frustrated but do not give up. Persevere day after day, week after week, month after month; it will be more than worth all the effort.

> Let's slow down and look at some of the benefits that can come from pursuing God together. There are a number of studies that help confirm these points. They also reflect my experience as a Christian counselor for over thirty years.
>
> Praying, reading the Bible, worshipping, and serving together all work to align you and your spouse both relationally and spiritually. Think about it: praying, reading the Bible, worshipping, and serving are all intimate and personal acts. Pursued together, imagine how they might strengthen your marriage!
>
> So now the question becomes:
>
> ***What are you going to do about it?***

None of us wants to be another divorce statistic. None of us wants to let our hopes and our dreams die in the place from which no marriage returns. The picture of divorce is not pretty. It never has been. Of course you can divorce and then start over with someone else, but what makes you think the next time will be any different? The stats on second marriages are worse than those of first marriages.[3]

Most people just repeat the same destructive patterns, but you do not have to be another divorce statistic. You can do something together that will make a lasting difference. You can pursue God together every day for the rest of your lives, and that will keep your names out of the "divorce statistics" page of your local newspaper.

Look around you. How many times do you see Mark and Patricia, Steven and Betty, Sharon, William, Robert and Linda, Jessica and Joseph, or Melissa and Kevin walking around? Let me answer for you. You see them a lot. A whole lot.

Let me take you back to Mark and Patricia. Remember? They were the couple who chose me as their fourth counselor, and I told them if they were to break their cycle, they needed a heart change. They left my office that day without booking a follow-up appointment. That is never a good sign. I didn't think they liked my answer, and they could much easier move on to counselor number five.

God never ceases to amaze me. He definitely has a plan for our lives, and when He is ready to move, He moves. Guess who ended up back on my couch six weeks later? Mark and Patricia. In the six weeks since we last met, a lot had happened. They did visit counselor number five (I was right about that one). He solved their present problem but offered nothing that would help them break the cycle. They were ready to learn more about this "heart change" thing that I mentioned the last time they were in to see me.

Together we began to work through the first step to a heart change. I asked them to make two lists. On the first list I wanted them to write every want and desire they could think of that stood

---

3. National Stepfamily Resource Center, http://www.stepfamilies.info/ stepfamily-fact-sheet.php, referenced in Maggie Scarf, "Why Second Marriages Are More Perilous," *Time*, October 4, 2013, http://ideas.time.com/2013/10/04/ why-second-marriages-are-more-perilous/.

between them and God. This is such a crucial part of the process. We began their lists together, and then I sent them home to finish them. I shared with them some of the things that were on my list. Things like my selfishness and my pride, my desire to have everyone like me, and the compromises I made to make that happen. (This is not a confession time, so that is all you get!)

The next week they brought their lists back. I could tell by looking over their lists with them that they were serious about this process, and I was jumping up and down with joy inside. They had not shared their lists with each other, so I asked them to do so. I had Mark share one thing and then Patricia, and we went back and forth till we covered every item. There were lots of tears and pauses and hesitations, but we made it. Then we gave those lists to God. Each handed over all the things that were blocking their relationship with God and, ultimately, with each other. It was a powerful cleansing.

What would be on your lists? Think about it and pray about it. Then begin to make your lists. Our tendency is to hold back in one or two areas, but this does not work until you come 100 percent clean. Take whatever time you need. When you are finished, share your lists with each other. Some of you may be fine doing this as a couple, while others may want to do this with a pastor or counselor. Just do whatever it takes to successfully complete step one.

The next step was a logical and natural progression from step one. *Put God first in everything.* It is a simple commitment, but the most important commitment you can make after you ask Christ to be your Savior.

Step three is keeping God first every day for the rest of our lives. I asked Mark and Patricia to spend the next week discussing together what those steps meant for them individually and in their marriage.

Action Steps

Step One: Make a list of every want and desire that stands between you and God.

Share your lists and then in prayer give them to God

Step Two: Commit together to put God first in everything beginning today.

Seek His help together.

Step Three: Commit to keep God first in everything every day for the rest of your lives.

Daily seek God and pray for each other.

What does putting God first in everything mean to you? To me it means that God is now my filter that I run everything through. Big decisions go through God. Little decisions go through God. My thought life goes through God. God is my CEO, and daily I run His company that bears my name. It is a great deal. The pressure is off. He is in control, He wants what is best for me, He has an incredible plan for my life, and He always shows up. Deal.

Putting God first every day for some is a one-time event that lasts the rest of their lives, but for many others it is a process that we repeat over and over, day after day. Most of us have been living with God on the outside for a long time. Even though that is not where God wants to be, many of us have become comfortable with keeping Him in that position; but comfortable never changes anything. For things to change, God has to live on our inside, and living with Him on the inside is very different. It is literally life-changing.

Sometimes in this process we slip, and sometimes we fall; but we need to always put Him back in first place. It gets easier as we go along because we begin to see the benefits of living life His way. You know, sometimes I wonder why I ever put Him on the outside. My ways never work very well, and His always do. I guess I can just be a slow, stubborn learner at times.

For your life and for your marriage, make the decision to put God first, and then with His help, keep Him where He belongs. As transformative as this will be in your personal life, the truth is putting God first can be just as transformative in your marriage. As Nancy and I have learned, every change He has made in us and in our marriage has been better than we could have imagined.

It's decision time again.

First, you have to make the choice to stop the insanity. Second, you must choose to pursue God or not. It is all laid out for you.

All you need to do is say yes, and if that is your answer, I will see you in the next chapter—where we'll learn how to truly connect with our spouse.

CONNECT

The Art of Listening and Being Present

Putting God first in your marriage creates an environment for success. That is where God wants to be, and that is how He designed it to work. Then God makes it clear that the marriage relationship is the second most important relationship we have in this life. More important than other family members. Even more important than your kids, which we'll get to later. Keeping our focus on God puts our priorities where they need to be. In other words, He designed for us to connect with each other.

Often couples who connect so well while dating can find themselves as strangers just a few years into their marriage. Tom and Sarah found themselves in that challenging place.

From the first time I met them I thought that they were a special couple. Tom and Sarah were attending a new preparing-for-marriage class that I was teaching. They stood out not just because they were sitting in the front row but because they just seemed to get it. They saw the bigger picture. They understood that a good marriage would take a lot of work, and they already knew that God had to come first. They always showed up to class early and often stayed after class to ask questions. I remember telling them that if they worked as hard at marriage as they were working at preparing for it, they would have the marriage they both wanted.

It was almost seven years later that I got a call one day at my office from Sarah. She asked me if I remembered her and Tom, and when I said yes, she broke down in tears and said they were about ready to give up on their marriage. Now, I have been counseling people for a long time and nothing much surprises me, but this call from Sarah did. What in the world had happened to this couple who at the start seemed on the right track to build a successful marriage?

A couple of days later, they came to my office. As a counselor I look at the nonverbals because body language can reveal a lot. As they sat down on my couch, Tom hugged one end and Sarah the other. They did not look at each other, and the tension between them was almost visible. Honestly, if they had walked in without identifying themselves, I am not sure that I would have recognized them. They were not the same couple who had sat in the front row of my class seven years before.

As we talked and unpacked the past seven years, they'd had no major marriage-altering event. No affair. No pornography. No abuse. No addictions. Instead I saw a series of baby steps that took them away from each other over a long period of time. Tom got a promotion and spent more time at work and less time at home. Sarah had two babies, and when she quit her job to stay at home, the kids became her priority.

When they were together, the time was usually kid-focused, and by the time they hit the bed at night, both were exhausted. I asked them about their sex life, and they could not remember the last time they had been together physically. There were no dates, no romance, no connection, no communication. The slide from the mountaintop to the bottom had taken time, but they were now there and had no hope that things would change.

Tom and Sarah were somewhat unique as a premarital couple, but seven years into marriage, their story was one I hear often from couples married seven, ten, fifteen, and twenty-five years or more. Life happens, and because they quit communicating in the day to day, they lose connection.

In God's design for marriage, as we learned in the last chapter, He wants to be at the center. Ecclesiastes 4:12 says, "A cord of three strands is not quickly broken." I believe this is the husband, the wife, and God knit together so tightly that they cannot be broken apart. Two things happened to Tom and Sarah. They quit putting God first, and each quit putting the other second. Simply, the cord unraveled, and instead of fighting for their marriage, they began to fight each other.

Connecting Versus Coexisting

If you've had any exposure whatsoever to marriage resources, you know what experts say is essential over and over again: communication. Of the couples I see in counseling, the ones who really communicate well and set aside time to do so seem to consistently also have good marriages.

But in all this hype about communication, here's what is often missed: communication does not simply mean the talking kind. It means connection in a special way. It was clear that Tom and Sarah, as they sat coldly apart in my office, had lost their connection somewhere along the way.

Most couples communicate pretty well before marriage. I have seen surveys that usually put that number at around three hours a day. On the other hand there are surveys that say those same couples a few years into marriage will spend an average of five minutes a day communicating.[1] What happens? The reasons may vary from couple to couple, but the bottom line is that we quit making it a priority. We lose sight of God's design.

When Nancy and I were in college, we began dating halfway through Nancy's freshman year. At Texas Christian University, there were still dorm hours for the girls. That meant that the girls had a curfew. The guys did not, but the system worked. If

---

1. Bella DePaulo, "What Married and Single People Do Differently," Living Single, *Psychology Today*, March 20, 2014, http://www.psychologytoday.com/blog/living-single/201403/what-married-and-single-people-do-differently.

the girls were in, the guys went in. On our dates we would wait until the last minute before curfew—I got the evil eye more than once from the dorm mother as I rushed Nancy in the door just before it was closed and locked for the night. I would then hurry back to my room to call her on the phone (pre-cell-phone era), and we would talk for hours. That went on for two years. Then we got married.

Once we lived together, I would go to work, come home, have dinner, watch TV, spend time with Nancy, and go to bed. I think because we could be together more, we did not work as hard at communicating. Communication time shrank. I did not have to work at finding time to be with Nancy. She was there. She was there in the morning. She was there at night. She slept by my side. The changes in our communication patterns were so subtle that we did not realize they were taking place. We had been close and connected for a long time. Our communication had been great. She was my best friend and I was hers. Now a few years into marriage, we were beginning to feel like strangers.

There will always be distractions in life that keep us from connecting. Some are good and some are not. Some are necessary and some we choose.

There will always be distractions in life that keep us from connecting. Some are good and some are not. Some are necessary and some we choose.

In the early days of our marriage, I often chose to spend my time on work, TV, tennis, and hanging out with friends. None were bad in and of themselves, but Nancy no longer felt she was important. She was not always my number two.

Nancy's schedule was different from mine. She was finishing college and had a lot of free time. She was now a married student who went to class and then came home. She was bored, missed her TCU college friends, and was not as happy as she thought she would be. In her evaluation, it was my fault.

At that point, we should have turned to each other and said let's get back on track. We could have worked together to figure this early marriage thing out. We could have, but we did not. Instead of embracing our differences and dealing with them, we embraced the distractions and slowly stepped away from each other. Our communication that was so good before marriage got worse and worse. We were morphing into the thirty-five-minutes-a-week communication statistic. Things needed to change, or this marriage would end in disaster.

How connected are you today with your spouse? Are you more connected than ever, or are you becoming strangers? Think about a typical day and the things that you do. How do you spend your time? How much time do you set aside to connect with your spouse?

I can sit in the same room or on the same couch with Nancy and not be connected. Just being in each other's presence does not connect us. Sure, it helps. The opportunity is there, but to connect, someone has to initiate. That initiation may be a conversation, or it could be a hug or a kiss. Connection happens when one initiates and the other one responds. So you have to make a choice in how to spend your time together.

Most nights during the workweek, I get home around 6:30 p.m. My days are long. I start at 5:30 a.m. by rolling (often literally) out of bed and having some time with God. Then I head to the gym to work out, come back home to get ready, and head to the office. By the time I walk in the house in the evening, I can be pretty tired.

Now this is where I have some choices. Let's look at two options. Option one: I can sit down to relax. After all, I have worked all day and I deserve this time to myself. Watching TV or listening to music helps me unwind and distracts me from the pressures of the day. Usually by 7:00 p.m. or so, we have dinner. It is nice to have a quiet dinner or maybe continue watching a show I have gotten interested in. After dinner, we usually watch something together. By nine thirty or ten, I am ready to head to bed. Nancy usually follows me pretty soon after, but sometimes I am asleep before she gets to the bedroom.

The next day and the next and the next can all be repeats. Same pattern. Same unconnected time together, and eventually we realize that we are just coexisting. We are not fighting, but we sure are not connecting. We are unconnected.

And unconnected couples can become strangers.

Option two: I come in the house at 6:30 p.m. and the first thing I do is find my wife. This is not a Lewis and Clark thing. I can usually find her in the kitchen, her office, or the back part of our house. Then I do one of my favorite things. I hug her and give her a kiss, and you know what? That hug and kiss energize me. They usually do much more for me than watching TV or listening to music. Someone told me years ago that the first five minutes a couple is together in the evening sets the tone for the night. Taking time to connect makes a difference.

We then usually spend time talking and catching up on each other's day. We always have dinner together and like watching something together we both want to see. I have no problem with a couple watching a show or movie together. We are experiencing the same thing and can interact on it. Then we can get each other's take on what we have both seen. We connect. Usually I am the first to head to the bedroom, but I wait for Nancy so we can pray together. We connect. Then even as we go to sleep, we are always touching. It may be our feet or our hands or cuddling. We connect.

Two options, and a number of choices. If we consistently choose option two, we stay connected. We are both initiating and both responding. Something else I find interesting: When I choose option one, I am often still tired the next morning. When I choose option two, I usually wake refreshed and energized. I believe it is the connection. God designed us for relationships—a relationship with Him and a relationship with others. When we connect in marriage with our spouse, we are fulfilling God's design for our lives; and it makes a difference.

How about setting aside some time with your spouse to talk about connecting? Tell each other when you feel the most connected. Share how connected you feel in your marriage today. Is this where you want to be? If it is, great. Keep on doing what you are doing. If not, what will you do today to connect? (Actually, if you are talking about this, you have already taken a step!)

Let's Talk About Silence

We had been married about six weeks, and Nancy wanted to attend the wedding of one of her sorority sisters in Fort Worth. I agreed to go with her but was not overly excited about spending my weekend at a wedding event. Nancy, on the other hand, was looking forward to going back to TCU. Many of her friends were still there and would be at the wedding.

I took off work that Friday so we could leave early. When we were packing for the trip, we had an argument. Typical of important, life-changing arguments, I have no idea what it was about. I just know I wanted my way about something and was not getting it. I said, "Fine, then I am not going to Fort Worth with you." (I sometimes marvel at my high level of maturity!)

I went in the living room of our apartment, turned on the TV, and relaxed on the couch. I knew she would come around sooner or later. I would get my way, and we would be off on "her" trip.

An hour later she came out of the bedroom, but not with the countenance I had hoped for. In her hand was the phone, one of those phones with a cord. She said, "The phone is for you." I said, "I didn't hear it ring." She said, "It didn't. It's your mother, and I called her! I told her how you were acting." I could not believe it—my bride of six weeks had thrown me under the bus, and not just any bus, but one driven by my mother who, up until then, thought I was almost perfect.

I do not remember exactly what my mother said, but her words were few and very clear. We were soon on the way to Fort Worth—together. That was the last time I pouted and used the silent treatment with Nancy. My actions had shut the door to communication and put my desires ahead of her. And God? I had taken Him off my radar.

I learned the hard way that silence also communicates—loud and clear. My silent treatment communicated to Nancy that she did not matter as much as what I wanted. What does silence mean to you? In some homes, silence meant that someone was mad and eventually things would explode.

Maybe you survived by lying low and staying out of the line of fire. In other homes, silence may have been a sign that all was well, and the family was enjoying a time of tranquility. Now, put a guy from the first home with a girl from the second home into a new marriage situation and what do you get? You get a big problem. The husband interprets her silence as anger, and the wife interprets his silence as "everything is fine." Talk about a connection misfire!

Whether it is purposeful or not, silence communicates—and you have to know what it means to your spouse.

The "silent treatment" can create an unhealthy atmosphere for a marriage of confusion and uncertainty. Chad loved Lori and had for a long time. They were high school sweethearts, went their separate ways in college, and then in their early twenties reunited and married. One of the things that always amazed Chad about their relationship was that it was fight-free. Three years in high school and another year of dating before marriage and not one fight.

Whether it is purposeful or not, silence communicates—and you have to know what it means to your spouse.

His friends said just wait, but Chad knew differently. This was the perfect relationship. Besides, Lori had this amazingly sweet personality. She never raised her voice and never used harsh words. Chad thought they were home free.

Chad first came to see me by himself. He thought he was crazy. By this time they had celebrated three anniversaries. Things were still good, or at least he thought they were, but something new was added to their relationship that just did not seem to fit. Chad told me that they still had not had a fight; at least he did not think they had. Yet things were different.

Lori was quiet by nature, but now Chad realized there were times when she was too quiet. I asked him for an example. He told me about a recent time when two of his friends had invited him to go on a weekend hunting trip. Lori told Chad that it was not a problem when he asked, but then he began to think that it was. For the next few days, Lori barely spoke to him, hardly ever looked him in the eyes, and slept as far away from him as their bed would allow. But when he asked her if anything was wrong, he always got the same answer. "No."

The silent treatment, now that Chad thought about it, had began the previous week, when Lori had taken Chad to look at a new couch she was interested in. Chad liked the couch but also paid the bills and knew they could not make a purchase that large right then. Lori said she understood, but then commenced her silence. In fact, as Chad relayed these stories to me, he realized that the silent treatment had become a part of their marriage.

I asked him if it was working for Lori. He said no, but then told me he had canceled the hunting trip, and they had bought the couch. So much for "not working."

Chad's definition of a fight was a loud one. Lori's definition of a fight was a quiet one. This was where they encountered their disconnect. Quiet was winning the fights, but the marriage was beginning to lose. That is the irony. Just because something works in our mind does not mean that it is healthy for the marriage. Silence can be healthy. The silent treatment is not. The silent treatment can scream in what it communicates, and when it does, red flags should begin to pop up all over the place.

Don't be fooled by quiet. Recognize that there is a problem and begin the process of getting help. Silence can communicate a number of things in a marriage. Only you can decide if it is healthy or not.

Three Keys to Connecting Well

The foundation of successful communication is first and foremost found in looking in the mirror. How does your spouse view you? What are the qualities that you possess as a spouse? All of this informs how your spouse will frame you in his or her mind, and it's to your own advantage to keep this in mind when you're not connecting. Then use that perspective to take a closer look at why.

I have always wanted to be someone whom Nancy trusted, to have her feel safe with me. I wanted to be so positive in her mind that even when I blew it in communication, she could still see me as a trustworthy person to whom she wanted to be married.

Maybe you feel the same way.

As we take this hard, close look in the mirror to see what our spouse sees in us, I've found three qualities are particularly worth paying attention to.

The first is compassion. Compassion is accomplished through acceptance. It is the acceptance of another's thoughts, feelings, and actions. It is letting them be who God created them to be and not trying to change them into who we want them to be.

It took Nancy and me a long time to get this. I used to blame it on getting married young, but over the years I have seen people trying to change their spouse all the way to the retirement home. I grew up in a healthy, loving family. My parents deeply loved each other and were great role models. Nancy's growing-up years in a dysfunctional home were difficult. It made perfect sense to me that my family should be our model. However, Nancy did not exactly see it that way—especially when I was trying to change her!

Meanwhile, Nancy was trying to change me too. She put her dad on a pedestal. He was athletic and I was not. He was the life of the party and I was not. I could go on and on, but since I am writing this, I do not have to throw myself under the bus. She became critical of me because I did not fit her mold. So she spent years trying to change me. It never worked.

Think about it for a minute. Do you want someone to come

into your life and try to change you into the person they want you to be, or do you want someone in your life who loves you and accepts you as you are? That is compassion, and the acceptance it brings to a marriage will literally change the relationship. Nancy wanted me to accept her thoughts, feelings, and actions. She wanted to be able to tell me everything and have no fear of judgment. She wanted me to be able to love her as she was and let God make the changes in her that He wanted to make. I did not do that at first. In fact, I did not do that for a long time.

Today I am better at it. Today she is better at it, and do you know what we discovered? That was God's plan all along. God will never make me into anyone who is not perfect for Nancy or her into anyone not perfect for me. He values marriage too much. He wants our marriage to succeed and to be fulfilling. Whatever He does to bring about change in my life or hers will help accomplish that purpose.

So accept each other. Accept your differences because you have them. You know something I have learned as a counselor sitting across from couples all these years? God NEVER puts two people together who are alike. NEVER. And to bridge those immense differences, you need compassion. You are different so you can grow and challenge each other and be able to say after fifty years of marriage that your life was so much better because you were married to him or married to her. Embrace your differences. Accept each other just as you are, and add compassion to your marriage.

The second key to understanding how our spouse sees us is authenticity. It is not just what we say; authenticity is about how we say it. It is building a relationship over time that lets your spouse know that what you say is real and sincere. It is the assurance that you never have lied to or deceived your spouse, nor ever will. It is a combination of integrity, honesty, and a desire to honor God with your life. It is an incredible foundation that is rock solid.

Let's stop for a minute, because I don't want to lose you. I can hear some of you saying, "I have already blown it. Is there hope for me?" The answer is yes, and here is why. I have blown it, too. In fact, I do not know anyone who has not blown it at one time or another in their marriage, but that is not a reason to lower the standard.

If we begin to say this is okay or that is okay when they are not, what have we accomplished? We have just dumbed down marriage and devalued God's plan. Even though it is high and difficult to attain, the standard needs to remain where God places it. We are all going to mess up at one time or another. When it happens, be quick to acknowledge your mistake, and then learn from it.

Remember this: married life is a lot like being in a boot camp. Marriage is a time of learning and growing and figuring out how to honor God with our lives. At times the going is tough. Your spouse knows that you will not be perfect, or if they do not, they need to accept that fact. Nancy knows that I am not perfect. Yet she also wants to know that I am daily letting God mold me into who He wants me to be. When I blow it today, I quickly acknowledge what I did and take full responsibility. That is not easy.

I used to acknowledge wrongs quickly but had trouble taking full responsibility for my actions. That needed to change. Then I asked God what He wanted me to do differently and what I needed to learn out of the experience. That put things in a different perspective. My accountability was now to God. That made a difference in me and in my marriage. That built a foundation of genuineness.

The final key is empathy. In the Bible, Jesus talks to us about being servants. My impression is that this is both in our actions and in our attitudes. For me, it means putting my selfish desires aside and putting Nancy before myself. It is that God-first, spouse-second thing again. For me, empathy involves asking myself two questions. First, no matter what the situation, I want to look at it from Nancy's perspective. I ask myself, "Exactly what is her perspective?" Then the game changing question for me is, "How is her perspective different from mine?"

When I take the time to ask those two questions, I connect

better with Nancy. I am taking the time to "walk in her shoes" and taking the time to see how our perspectives are different. Then my response draws us together. She knows I care, and she knows I have taken the time and made the effort to understand her. The more I do this, the better our marriage.

Being empathetic can also have an economic impact. A few years ago, I was getting ready for work one morning. On this particular day, I was running a little late—not a lot, but a little bit. I had finished showering and was drying off. Nancy was also getting ready. The home we lived in at that time was a product of the late 1960s, and we had a rather small master bathroom—especially when we were both trying to get ready at the same time. As I began to get dressed, I saw Nancy looking at the baseboard around the shower. Now, my wife sells homes, and she takes her work very seriously. She also feels it is her obligation to make sure our home is free from all of the hazards and maladies that she sees in the homes that she shows. We are protected from termites and bugs and water leakage.

Once, many years ago, she was sure that we had termites in our basement. She got our son Grant and a hammer, and they began ripping paneling off the basement walls to find hidden termites—which were not there. So, when I saw that look in her eyes again that morning, I should have been more "empathetic." I should have taken the time to look at it from her perspective and then see how that perspective differed from mine.

Nancy was soon on her hands and knees pulling back the baseboard. She said, "I think we have black mold. Look. Do you see it?" As I said before, I was running a little late so I said, "Honey, I would not know black mold if it hit me in the face. Get someone to look at it, and do what you need to do." That was definitely not taking the time to be empathetic. I didn't look at things from her perspective.

That was about eight in the morning. I left for work and had a busy day unfolding before me. That evening around 6:30 p.m.,

I walked back in the house. As expected, it had been a difficult day, and I was exhausted. Nancy and I had not talked all day, and she was not home when I got there. I walked upstairs into our bedroom and was blocked from going into the bathroom—my bathroom—by blue tape that crisscrossed the doorway. My shower was gone. The tile floor was gone—the bathroom had been gutted in the past ten hours.

I guess I thought that Nancy would get someone out to look at the mold—if it was indeed mold—and spray something on it. The mold would be gone. I would tack the baseboard back in place and that would take care of the dreaded "black mold epidemic" in our house. The truth is I had not given it a second thought since 8:01 a.m. that morning. I had failed to ask myself the important questions of empathy: How does Nancy look at this situation, and how is that different from how I look at it? In her mind, I had given her the green light. She saw the problem and attacked it. I know this about my wife but did not take the time to think it through on this occasion. The silver lining in the story: a few thousand dollars later, I had a nice, brand new shower that I liked.

> Compassion, authenticity, and empathy work together to lay the foundation of how your spouse views you. When I am totally in sync with these, I am on solid ground in my marriage.

When was the last time you tried to put yourself in your spouse's shoes? There are opportunities every day to do this. Start today. Ask God to show you an opportunity to be empathetic. Then do it. You will be amazed at the results.

So compassion, authenticity, and empathy work together to lay the foundation of how your spouse views you. When I am totally in sync with these three, I am standing on solid ground in my marriage. Nancy experiences me accepting her unconditionally. She trusts what I tell her and knows that I would never knowingly do something to hurt her. Finally, the empathy I show lets her know that I have taken the time to walk in her shoes.

No matter where your marriage is today, take time to look in the mirror. Ask yourself these questions. What does your spouse see? How are they interpreting your words and actions? What needs to change?

As you begin to work on compassion, acceptance, and empathy, you will become aware of two minor miracles. You are placing your spouse firmly in the position God wants you to have him or her, and it keeps you building an awesome marriage. Those alone make that long look in the mirror worth it.

Learning the Art of Listening

Once I became aware of the importance of empathizing with Nancy, I found lots of opportunities to do so. Nancy likes to go to parties. When an invitation arrives, it goes on the refrigerator door. The date is circled on the calendar and I am informed about this great event that we can look forward to together. I, on the other hand, do not like parties. I started to say hate, but that was too strong. The truth of how I feel about most parties lies somewhere between "not like" and "hate." I have learned over the years that because parties are important to Nancy, they need to also be important to me. I have improved and have learned to enjoy watching her have fun, and every once in a while, I have fun too.

It had been a grueling week. I seemed to never get on top of things, and each day as I opened the refrigerator to get some orange juice for breakfast, I was reminded of the party we were going to together on Friday night. By the time Friday evening came around, I was a walking zombie and was pretty grumpy to top it off. As I came in the house, I found my wife ecstatic. She had just gotten a new manicure and pedicure and arrived home just before me. I managed a "hey" and followed her to the bedroom to get ready.

As I got out of my new shower, Nancy was standing there holding up a dress, and her entire expression had changed. "I sent this dress to the cleaners two weeks ago so that it would be ready for tonight. It has a spot on it and the cleaners is closed, and even if they were open, they could not fix it in time."

This presented a great opportunity for me to step up as a husband. In this one scenario, I had the opportunity to be authentic, to show compassion, and to be empathetic. By listening to what she was saying and responding in a way that connected us, I could show her how important she was to me.

Though, maybe like you, I'm a bit of a slow learner. Instead I said, "You could wear something else or just wear that. It will probably be dark in there tonight anyway." Now most of the guys reading this are saying, "Right on. You nailed it." But hold on, I did not.

I did not listen to Nancy. I jumped in to fix the problem. This seems to be one of the curses of man in marriage. Nancy needed me to acknowledge her hurt. Sure, in my perspective it was just a dress and just a party, but to her, this was important, and she had communicated that very well to me.

I should have used a different approach: "Honey, I am sorry. I know you have been looking forward to this party and planned well for it. You have to be disappointed." Bingo. That would have connected us. That was what she was looking for and needed. Then she may have asked me to help her figure out a solution, but first I needed to connect with her.

Listening to your spouse can make or break your connection. I like to call the listening that grows your marriage "connective listening." It is interesting that those who study listening tell us that most of us can think and process others' words five times faster than they can speak. Do you know the implications of that? When Nancy is talking, I have a lot of extra time to think. If I focus on what she is saying and what she needs from me, things will go well. If I spend that extra time thinking about what I am going to do when she finishes or what I am going to say in retort, things will not go well. She will not feel listened to, and, more importantly, she will not feel connected.

By listening, I don't mean merely hearing a person's words come out of their mouth. I mean connective listening—truly, intentionally seeking to understand and connect to your spouse. If I listen to Nancy, I am also connecting with her. This kind of listening goes beyond hearing the words to hearing her heart. What is she feeling? What is she trying to get me to hear? How do I respond so she feels heard?

All of these considerations are a part of listening to her in a way that connects us. If she tells me that she is tired but still needs to go to the grocery store, what will my response be?

I could say, "I am sorry you are tired, but it shouldn't take you that long." I would have heard her words and responded, and she would have gone on to the store, but we wouldn't have connected.

Instead, I could say, "Why don't I go with you? I will drive and help you shop." Again, I would have heard her words about shopping but also addressed her need because she was tired. The end result is the same with both. The groceries get bought, but we connect in the second scenario.

Communication without connection is common in marriages. When I listened to Grace and Kyle tell their story, it was pretty apparent neither one was listening to the other. Grace came out of a family that did not listen well. They were all overachievers and did not have the time to listen. Her dad set the tone, and the rest of the family fell into place.

Grace honestly thought she was listening and responding to what Kyle said, but it simply was not working. They seldom—if ever—really connected. Kyle, on the other hand, grew up in a very close family that communicated well. They picked up on each other's body language and tone of voice. They were sensitive to each other in a healthy, caring way.

One situation in Kyle's high school years demonstrated this support. He had played football. He was good and aimed to be the starting quarterback his senior year. Kyle attended a large high school with a lot of good, competitive athletes. Fall practice began at the end of summer with two-a-days. The tradition was to name the starting quarterback at the end of the two-a-days stint. Practices were going well, and Kyle knew it was between him and another senior, Lee.

Kyle came in the house late one afternoon after the announcement. His dad was home early that day, and his first question to Kyle was, "Well, are you the new starting quarterback?" Kyle tried to answer, but the words would not come; he could only shake his head "no." His dad's response demonstrated—in neon lights—the differences in listening between the homes Kyle and Grace grew up in. His dad said, "Ouch. That must hurt. I'm so sorry. I love you and just know you will turn this into something good for you. Your mom and I will not miss a game."

Kyle went to practice the next Monday and practiced harder than ever. He made a decision to enjoy practice, and as he ran the scout team each week, he did an incredible job playing the role of the opposing quarterback. All that resulted from a connecting, listening response from his dad.

And it paid off—the week before the state playoffs began, the starting quarterback was injured and out for the rest of the season. But the team didn't miss a beat, as Kyle stepped in and led them to the state championship.

Kyle carried those listening skills into marriage, but Grace never learned them the way he had. He was trying to connect through listening, but it seemed for Grace listening was just a means to an end. "Tell me what you want and I will do it." "If I tell you what I want, do it."

Grace's idea of listening was functional but did nothing to connect them. Over time Kyle grew weary of trying to connect and began to listen like Grace listened. They never fought. Things got done. They listened without connecting, and now they just went through the motions in their marriage. As we talked, they agreed that they wanted more.

I tried to use a different word with Grace. One that might

resonate different from "listening." I talked to them about focus. Where was their focus when listening? If the focus was functional, they were succeeding. If the focus was connecting, they were failing. That seemed to make sense, and Grace said, "I want to connect." She saw that functional listening could not give her what she was missing in her marriage. The pieces began to fit

> **If you choose to listen as a means of connecting, things can be different for you and your marriage.**

together. Grace saw a new path, and Kyle was willing to put in the effort again. Their marriage could be different, and they were excited about all that the future held for them.

You may have all kinds of reasons for not listening to your spouse. You may not have the time. You may not understand his or her feelings. A number of things could get in the way. As long as you stay stuck, you will never build the marriage that God put in your heart. If you choose to listen as a means of connecting, things can be different for you and your marriage, too. Connective listening lets your spouse know you care, showing how greatly you value her or him. It puts your spouse in the number two position—after God—and helps keep that priority. It takes both of you working together to make this happen.

Can you see what a difference this can make for your marriage? Ask God for His help, and start listening in a connecting way today.

Stop, Look, Listen

Remember Tom and Sarah, the premarital counseling superstars whose light faded as they began life together? If their communication were to be judged on talking alone, they were doing quite well. They talked all the time—exchanging words about schedules, kids' activities, who was going to pick up milk and bread, and other daily needs. Yet when it came to *connecting* on an intimate level, they were failing miserably. They didn't talk about their interpersonal issues at all.

In fact, they'd stopped trying.

I asked Tom and Sarah if they remembered the "Stop-Look-Listen" communication tool that they had learned from me in class. Tom said, "Yeah. We got good at that and it made a difference, but we quit using it." I asked him if it quit working for them, and Tom said, "No. We just stopped." It was time to begin using it again.

"Stop-Look-Listen" is a great way to bring connective listening into your marriage.

Suppose Nancy wants to talk to me about something that is important to her. How can I make her a priority?

First, I need to STOP everything else that I am doing.

That means turning off the TV (not just putting it on mute) or putting down the book, smartphone, or whatever else could distract me from listening to her. For me, it has to be stopping everything but breathing.

Then I need to LOOK at her. Make eye contact. Face her. Be conscious of my body language. Relax.

Finally, I need to LISTEN to every word she says and be able to verbally let her know that I heard her.

When I follow these steps, I have accomplished connective listening.

Here is an example from our life. It is Saturday afternoon, and I am sitting in my favorite chair in our living room. It is football season, and I have set aside this afternoon to flip through as many games as I can. I am totally zoned out. Enter Nancy. She says she needs to talk. What should I do? Now, I teach this stuff, and I know what to do, but that does not always make it easy. I could put football into Nancy's place in priority and say "later," and there was a time when I might have made that decision, but today is not that day.

So I stopped. I turn the TV off. OFF. Not down. Not on mute. I turned it off.

Then I looked. As Nancy sits down, I turn and face her. She tells me that her dad just called and that they are taking her sister, who lives in Texas, to Houston for some medical tests. Her sister has always been healthy, but I sense concern in Nancy's voice as she tells me she wants to wait until the first tests are run; and then, if they are not good, she wants to fly to Houston. She also would want me to go with her.

Finally, I let her know I was listening. Now it is my turn. I say, "I'm sorry. I love your sister too. Of course, we will go."

That was a home run! I heard her. Her countenance softened because she knew that I listened and that I understood. We connected in a way that we wouldn't have if I had left the TV on.

Stop–Look–Listen

STOP everything you are doing.

LOOK with your entire body.

LISTEN actively to every word your spouse says.

You can use "Stop-Look-Listen" for everything from deciding where to go for dinner to connecting on a deep emotional level. The more you use this model, the more natural it becomes. Keep it in your "we are going to have an awesome marriage" toolbox and use it daily.

Now STOP. If you don't take time to try this out now, it will get lost in that pile of things you know are good for your marriage but you never do.

So here goes. Each of you write down three things you would like to share with the other that are important to you. Maybe it is something you would like the two of you to do together. Maybe it is something that is concerning you that you want the other's input on. Maybe you are tired of Mexican food every time you go out to dinner. I don't care what is on your list as long as it is important to you. There is not a right list and a wrong list, for those of you who are wondering! Now take turns sharing the things on your list. Lady first. Share your first item. Then the guy takes a turn, and then alternate till you finish.

I gave this assignment to another couple I was counseling, Allen and Robin. They made their lists and decided they would set aside time the next Saturday morning to share. As Allen walked into the kitchen, he remarked about how quiet the house was that morning. Robin reminded him of the STOP part of their exercise. Everything was off, including the dishwasher, which always ran on Saturday morning.

They sat down together at their breakfast table, faced each other, and took deep breaths. This was not easy for either one of them. Allen felt a twinge of fear, and Robin had been awake since 5:00 a.m. Robin went first. "Allen, you have been working a lot of extra hours lately. I am proud of you and how well you are doing. I know to advance and meet your goals you have to work hard, and I totally support you in that. My problem is that I miss you, and I would like to see if we could set aside a night each week for a date for just the two of us. It would help me a lot, and hopefully it would be good for you, too."

We can learn from Robin's approach here. She complimented Allen. She made sure that he knew she was on his team. Then she stated her need without making him defensive and left it open for him to respond.

Allen thought for a moment, looked her in the eyes, and said, "I know my job has affected you and us. I don't want you to suffer because of my job. I miss us too. I want to spend time with you. I don't want to lose my incredible wife. I am totally onboard with your idea. How about we try Saturday nights?" (I could not have scripted it any better.) He started out by connecting with her and letting her know he heard her, then he responded with a plan of action.

Stopping, looking, and listening are not always our most natural responses, if we're honest. They can be inconvenient, certainly. You may feel you don't have the time. But I'm confident that if you give it a try, you'll find what it can do for your marriage is more than worth it.

The Legacy of a Connected Marriage

So far I have given you examples of a number of couples that have come to see me. Now I want to tell you about a couple that I went to see. I believe that everyone needs a Paul and everyone needs a Timothy in their lives.

Paul lived at the time after Jesus. He was a guy that hated Christians. His job was to do away with them, and he did it effectively until one day Jesus came to him, confronted him, and changed his life forever. Paul spent the rest of his life telling people about Jesus.

Enter Timothy. Paul mentored Timothy. He spent time with him and invested in him so that Timothy could also spread the news about Jesus.

Enter me. I want to invest in others and teach them God's plan for marriage. I also want to learn from those who have followed that plan for a long time. I want to always have a Paul and a Timothy in my life. As a counselor, Timothy was easy, but I needed a Paul.

Enter Ernest and Phyllis. I watched this elderly couple at church a long time before I met them. They were there every week and usually sat in the same spot. Ernest was always mindful of Phyllis, and she was always appreciative. I didn't yet know them, but I could tell they were connected. I saw it in the way they treated each other and the way they looked at each other.

Finally, I introduced myself and asked them if Nancy and I could take them to lunch sometime. I was a little surprised that they immediately said yes. A week later, we met after church for lunch. It was an incredible two hours. This couple got it. They knew, understood, and lived out God's plan for marriage. They were married as teens and were now eighty-seven and eighty-five, respectively. They acted much younger than that, and clearly they'd never lost their spark.

As they shared their story, I was truly in awe. They'd had four children. One had died as an infant and another in her thirties from cancer, and two were still living. Ernest worked for a large company for a number of years and then went out on his own. He went broke and worked his way back into his old job. They were in good health now, but both had undergone surgeries in the past. The entire time we talked, they sat side by side holding hands. They lit up as they talked about their life together, and each smiled and listened as the other took a turn talking.

I finally asked them the question I'd been waiting to ask: "What is your secret?" Their answer was not some hidden secret that would change marriages forever. Instead, it was a rubber stamp of time-tested truths. The difference between Ernest and Phyllis and so many other couples was that they latched onto the truths and never let go. They connected, and the connection grew their marriage each year.

Ernest said, "When we started out, I don't think anybody besides Phyllis and me gave us much of a chance. We both had to work. Then Phyllis got pregnant a year into marriage. We were so excited. We made the spare room in our little house into a nursery and began planning for the baby. Bradley was born a month early and lived only three days. I think if he was born today they could have saved him. I never knew a person could hurt so bad. I couldn't imagine the hurt Phyllis felt, and I did not know what to do. We were at a crossroads. Neither of us was twenty yet, and our world was crumbling.

"Then, out of the blue, Phyllis's doctor's nurse invited us to come to her church. We were not against church but had just never taken time for it since we'd gotten married. We sure had nothing to lose, so we agreed. As I look back now, that Sunday was a miracle day for us. We walked into that church on a Sunday morning as low and empty as we could be, and a couple of hours later we walked out with hope. The sermon was fine, but that was not where God really touched us.

"As we headed to a Sunday school class, an older couple stopped us. They introduced themselves and asked us to come to the church kitchen and have coffee with them. This was the first time I ever knew God really cared about us. This couple shared their married life with us. They talked about their struggles and how close they came to giving up. Then they shared how they invited God into their lives and their marriage. It was not an overnight change, but things changed. Most of all they had a new direction, a new hope, and a plan for their marriage. They told us God had the same for us, and we believed them."

Then Ernest told me — the secret to their marriage: "We decided then and there that God was going to be the center of our marriage and that we were committing to His plan for us no matter what it was." That was the secret. That is what made the difference. That decision put them on the same page in the same book and had connected them for life.

We listened to story after story. We laughed and shed tears with them. Theirs was a living, breathing, awesome marriage. Later that afternoon, I kept thinking back to our time with Ernest and Phyllis. A few weeks before, I read a study about the effect good, connected relationships have on one's wellbeing. People can be healthier and happier. Life has more purpose and meaning. It made sense when I read it, and it really made sense after meeting Ernest and Phyllis.

> The secret to their marriage: "We decided then and there that God was going to be the center of our marriage and that we were committing to His plan for us no matter what it was."

Isn't the essence of life all about connecting? First we connect with God and then with a spouse. The difference is then evident in the life we lead and the life of the one we love.

Your Turn

When I walk around the mall or a public place with Nancy, I see lots of couples. I can usually tell pretty quickly if a couple is connected or not. Granted that a shopping trip may not always be the best time to judge a couple. (I give a guy a few points for just being at the mall with his wife.) When I see what I think is a connected couple, I get excited. I know they are experiencing what God wants for every couple in marriage. When I see couples who obviously have no connection at all, it saddens me because I know they are missing out on one of the greatest gifts God gives us in this life.

> ### *Where is your marriage today?*
>
> If you are connected, keep it up. Do not coast. Work at it every day. If you are not connected, why not turn it around? Start at the foundation: God first and spouse second.

When you talk to your spouse, don't leave it at a mere exchange of words. Try to connect. Try to truly listen and seek to understand what your spouse is saying to you.

Take time to make a list of all the things that are distractions in your marriage. Then take the steps necessary to keep your spouse a priority over each and every one of these distractions. Never forget that you are always communicating something to your spouse — even when you are silent. Build a foundation for great communication by working on compassion, authenticity, and empathy. Listen well; and, finally, make "Stop-Look-Listen" a natural part of your communication as a couple.

> ### *Remember, the only person you can change is yourself.*
>
> If you wait for your spouse to change first, you will run out of life. But if you change, maybe he or she will, too. It is worth taking the risk because if you do and your spouse responds, you may be one of those couples I see at the mall and think, "Now they are connected!" Wouldn't that be nice?

ENGAGE

How to Fight Right

The first time I remember my parents fighting, I was ten years old. The second and last time I remember them fighting, I was twelve years old. That's it. For the first eighteen years of my life I lived at home, and I only remember them fighting twice. My interpretation of this was that parents who loved each other did not fight. This would not serve me well later as I stepped into marriage.

It was not that I was naive about couples fighting. In my neighborhood, there was a couple down the block who fought all the time. As kids, we would hide and watch them fight. It was cheap entertainment. My hypothesis was only further confirmed by this couple: good couples do not fight and bad couples do. They were a bad couple, and my parents were a good couple. Simple enough.

While I was growing up in a fairly conflict-free home, my future wife was not. Nancy's parents did not fight all the time, but when they did, it was often extreme. What's more, they did not often resolve their issues, so they would keep coming back. It left a mark on Nancy that she unknowingly carried into marriage.

Over the two years that we dated, our fights were minimal. The couple of times they escalated came when we had been drinking (one of the hazards of college life for us), and we chalked those fights up to just that—drinking. We were great at analyzing our issues. The rest of our fights were typically selfish arguments that probably were never resolved because they were so petty.

Only years later did I realize the issues themselves were not our problem. It was the *way* we fought that was the problem. When you are dating and still have butterflies at the thought of each other, you can kiss and make up and tomorrow is a new day. We became experts at this conflict resolution method, never realizing that someday we would need to change.

As I bragged about our relationship before marriage, my few older acquaintances warned me that things would be different when Nancy and I were married and living together 24/7. I shrugged them off because I knew we would be different. They might have problems arise because they were married, but we would not. I came from a home without fighting and would establish a home without fighting. Nancy also wanted that, but we had no idea how our families of origin would affect our marriage.

I do not remember any of the specifics of our first big fight in marriage. I just remember internally swearing and thinking, "This is not good." The whole bad couple versus good couple paradigm flashed in my mind, and I was mentally moving us from category one to category two. I had no place else to put a fighting couple.

Fighting the Good Fight

The funny thing about my counseling work is that couples never come to see me because things are great in their relationship. They come to me because they're in the midst of a fight. And as Nancy and I had to learn, not all fighting is created equal.

Donna and Charles had been married fifteen years when they came to counseling because they "fought all the time." They weren't kidding, either. In the first hour that I was a part of their lives, they fought five times. They could not agree on the stories of their disagreements. I asked them to think of a time in their marriage when they did not fight. Both agreed there had been such a time; they just could not agree on when that time occurred.

As the session ended, I concluded that they really had fought most of the fifteen years of their marriage. That's a long time for unresolved issues to pile up. They fought about the same things over and over. No one gets married hoping to fight all the time. Neither did Donna and Charles. So how did they get into such a mess?

Ideally, a couple goes through all the steps to grow their marriage. They identify their insanities, they pursue God individually and together, and they learn to connect. This lays a foundation that is healthy and allows for growth. But Donna and Charles had never built that foundation.

Donna's mother was one of those black-and-white thinkers. Things were either right or wrong, and there was not a middle ground. In her mind, she spoke the truth because it was the truth. If the truth hurt, that was okay because in the big picture it needed to be said. Donna's relationship with her mom was great. She understood her mom and never doubted her mom's love for her or her motives behind anything she ever said to her. The small hurts were overshadowed by the bigger picture.

> **Ideally, a couple goes through all the steps to grow their marriage.... This lays a foundation that is healthy and allows for growth.**

Charles was sensitive. His mom and dad said he had always been that way. They accepted Charles for who he was and spent their time walking on eggshells around Charles as they raised him in their home. So when Charles fell in love in college, he fell hard. Charles wanted to marry her, but the girl was far from being ready for that kind of commitment. She did enjoy the money Charles spent on her, however.

She soon found that she could control Charles and get him to do whatever she wanted him to do. For Charles, it was easier to do what she wanted than to confront her. Besides, if he didn't, she could get a little mean, and that hurt. And he was not going to be hurt. The relationship lasted a little over a year until finally, Charles did get hurt—and it was over.

Donna seemed different when Charles met her. He felt he could let his guard down around her. And even though she could say some things that hurt him, she did it out of her love for him—or so she said. They dated and married. As Donna's love for Charles grew, so did her unbridled honesty. After all, her mother's honesty was always a sure sign that she loved Donna. But Charles didn't see it that way. As Donna became increasingly honest with Charles, the hurt got harder to take. Finally, Charles dug in and began fighting back.

There are times in a marriage when a husband or a wife needs to say things a spouse might not want to hear. But first you need to build such a strong foundation of love and trust that it is easy for each to speak truth into the other's life.

In our marriage, I value Nancy's input. I know she loves me deeply and always has my best interest at heart. Because of this, I would rather hear something I need to hear from her than from anyone else. Has it always been this way? Probably not, but over time we have built a relationship with this level of trust and openness.

This is a tough part of a healthy marriage for most couples. None of us ever embraces criticism. But if God wants me to hear something that will make my life and the lives of those around me better, I want to hear it from someone whom I trust and whose love for me overrides any fear of saying what needs to be said. In my life, that would be Nancy.

What about you and your spouse? Are you willing to say in love the tough things that sometimes need to be said? Have you built or are you building a foundation that allows for this type of openness and honesty? If you do not say these things, who will?

Forgiving Past Fights

Not only was Charles sensitive, but he also has a better memory than the smartest elephant. It's true of his entire life and certainly of the fifteen years of their marriage. This was one of the many reasons they never resolved issues; Charles never let go of anything. In the midst of any argument, Charles could bring up something Donna said or did from the past to bolster his case in the present. His arsenal was full of ammunition. He stored up every little thing Donna did wrong so that when it was time to fight, his arsenal was full of ammunition.

The problem with this strategy is that it keeps the marriage partners stuck in the past and unable to grow and progress together into the future. Dredging up the past and throwing it into the conflict of the present does not solve anything. In fact, it usually makes things worse.

The healthy model does not get stuck in the past, but moves forward: identify the problem, work it out, and move on — leaving the solved issue behind.

How often do you or your spouse drag the past into the present? Once an issue is resolved, can you leave it in the past? What unresolved issues are you facing now that you know will surface again sometime in the future? What would it take for you to resolve those issues now? What is your first step?

Choosing Your Words Wisely

Charles was hurt by Donna's honesty, so he took a defensive position. Where Donna's honest and truthful words to Charles were made in love, Charles's were not. As time went on, unkind words and motives just drove the wedge between them deeper and deeper. After all, how can you trust someone who actively stores up blame against you?

Think about your attitude toward your spouse. Are you critical? Are you quick to pass judgment? Do you hold on to grudges to use them in arguments at a future time? If you do, what is their response? Is that helping to build the marriage you want?

There are stacks of Bible verses that warn us of the dangers of the tongue—the words we speak. James 3:8 says, "But no human being can tame the tongue. It is a restless evil, full of deadly poison." That is a no-holds-barred warning that fit the times then and fits our times today. So ask God to help you speak words of love and life in your relationships, especially to your spouse.

Choosing Your Battles

As we rounded the curve and headed into year four of marriage, we had begun to fight about many things. We fought about what we said to each other and we fought about what we did not say to each other. We fought about what we were going to do and not do. We fought about the money we were going to spend and the money we were going to save. Some of the fights were short-lived and some lasted days.

Most of the time I could not remember this week what we fought about last week, but the damage remained. Fight piled upon fight, and we grew further and further apart. We didn't know how to choose our battles, so we simply fought them all. Something needed to change.

Choosing your battles is a very good fight strategy, and it goes like this. When something about your spouse bothers you, you have a choice to make. If it's worth addressing, you can work to resolve it—right then and there. However, there is a difference between talking it out with your spouse and fighting it out with your spouse. That's option one.

If you have never tried turning something over to God, pick out something you are struggling with and simply say, "God, I am giving this to You."

If it's a small thing, you can choose to let go of it. You just choose to not fight a battle. Congratulations!

Instead of holding on to it yourself, you can decide to turn it over to God. Some of you are thinking, "What in the world does turning it over to God mean?" Here is my take on that. I firmly believe in a God who cares about me and my life. He wants my marriage to be great, and His plan for my marriage beats my plan, big time.

God, then, is the filter I pass our conflict through. If something that Nancy does bothers me, I can say, "Okay, God, what do I do with this? Do I respond? Do I respond now? Do I let go of it? Do I let You take care of it, knowing whatever You do will be good for me and for my marriage?"

This is not an easy step for me, especially if I am irritated or angry (and at this point, I usually am). I would much rather take matters into my own hands and then let God clean up the mess I create afterward. I can be good at this process. Yet, no matter how good that may feel in the short term, it does not feel good in the long term and never accomplishes what I want for my marriage.

If you have never tried turning something over to God, try it now. Pick out something you are struggling with and simply say, "God, I am giving this to You. I need Your help and I need Your answer. Thanks."

Now comes the hard part. *Leave it with God.* I know. What if He did not hear you? He did. What if He does not act as quickly as you want Him to act? His timing is perfect. What if? Stop. Leave it with Him. I promise you, He will not let you down.

A New Fight Strategy

So what if God's answer is that you need to resolve the issue—and talk it out—with your spouse? There are a number of problem-solving methods. Ours is simple and it works. Let's go through the steps.

1. Pray that God will guide you through the process, and then agree with your spouse on a time and a place to discuss the problem.

This may seem simplistic, but I promise you from experience this is vital.

God always needs to be our first step. It allows us to calm down and invite Him into the process. He has the solutions we do not have on our own. We talked about praying together in an earlier chapter, so, for now, pray in whatever way is most comfortable for you.

The important thing is that you both involve God in the process. Then find the time and place that works. For many couples, meeting at a neutral place like a coffee shop or restaurant is helpful. This gets you away from the distractions that might be at home and also helps to keep the discussion calm.

When Nancy and I were trying to climb out of our hole of unresolved problems, we would make a time to talk without thinking it through. For example, one time we decided to talk after the kids were in bed. It was a great idea in theory, except that I was exhausted. Waiting for Nancy, I fell asleep minutes before we were to meet at 10:30 p.m. As you can imagine, this was not well received by my wife and only complicated the issue.

My next solution was to talk in the morning before the kids woke up the next day. I was willing to forgo my morning run to settle things between us. Nancy was not ecstatic about the idea since she is not an early morning person, but she reluctantly agreed. The next morning I realized the early time idea was a mistake. She was right, and this time was not going to work.

Solution: Sunday afternoon after taking the kids to a friend's house. It finally worked. That Sunday afternoon offered no distractions for either of us. The kids were at a safe place that they loved to be. Neither of us had another commitment, so the afternoon was ours.

If finding the right time and place to talk is not that important to you, look at it this way. What steps do you take if you need to have an important meeting with a coworker to solve a problem? You set a specific time to meet. Then you secure a place to meet and finally you make sure your schedule is cleared so there are no interruptions.

If I asked you if your marriage was as important to you as your work, most of you would say it is, and many of you would say it is more important. Doesn't taking the same steps to solve problems in marriage that you do in your work make sense? It can make the difference of whether you solve the problem or just complicate things all the more.

2. Agree on the problem with each of you taking responsibility for your part of the problem.

This step also came from our experiences. You would think that two pretty intelligent people involved in the same conflict would be able to agree on what they were fighting about. Guess what. Sometimes Nancy and I couldn't even agree on the source of our conflict.

Try this. Have one of you state the problem as you see it. Then the other can either agree or give their perspective. Sometimes it is simply semantics, and sometimes it is because there are actually two issues that need to be dealt with. If there are two issues, then you have two problems to solve. Separate them and take them one at a time.

Now comes a crucial part: taking responsibility. In all the years I have counseled couples, I have never seen a situation where both did not bear some responsibility. It might have been 1 percent to 99 percent, but both had a part in the problem. Usually it is pretty close to 50/50. By the time the conflict has played itself out, both of you have played a part. (Okay, I know there might be an exception, but that is not the point here.)

One of the issues that we dealt with as our kids became teenagers was curfews. Actually, the issue was not the curfew, it was how we were going to handle the kids when curfew was broken. I am going to give you way more information about myself than I should, but I think it will help me make a point.

As a teen, my curfew was usually around midnight. If there was something special going on, my parents usually let me stay out later. I almost always made my curfew—at least within five or ten minutes. The backstory is that there were nights I came in the front door, kissed my parents goodnight, went to my room, acted like I was going to bed, and slipped out my bedroom window.

If that was not bad enough, listen to this: I never got caught! It's not like I did this every weekend, but over a couple of years there were more times than I have fingers and toes to count them on.

Now, Nancy and I agreed on the times. We agreed on a five- or ten-minute grace period. We agreed that if curfew was broken, we would send the culprit to bed, and we would make our decision on discipline the next morning.

That was where things broke down. One of us became pretty lax on the discipline and the other was pretty strict. Guess who was lax? Right. The guy who never got caught. If I was up and someone came in late, I usually said go to bed and never mentioned to Nancy that someone had violated curfew. If Nancy was up and someone came in late, they were grounded on the spot for the next weekend.

Since neither one of us was doing what we agreed to, we were sending a mixed message to our kids. What's worse, neither of us knew what the other was doing. Nancy finally got wise when, on leaving for the evening, the kids began asking, "Who is waiting up for us tonight?" It was time to revisit the curfew issue, including consequences for breaking it. We both had responsibility in the failure of our initial plan, and it was going to take both of us working together to make a united stand before the kids.

How does this apply to you? My experience is that if both of you are not willing to take personal responsibility, you might as well stop here. You will never solve the problem.

3. Discuss possible solutions.

Evaluating different solutions was a difficult step for me. Since I help people solve their problems for a living, it only seemed logical to me that I would have the correct solution to solve every problem that we faced. But for some reason, Nancy did not see things this way at all. In grad school, I had a wise professor who told us that we needed to remember that we could never counsel our own family. Somewhere along the way, I forgot that piece of advice until Nancy politely reminded me of that truth.

Discuss solutions. Make a list. This is a great time to use Stop-Look-Listen. Take turns offering solutions. Whichever solution you choose to try, both of you need to get behind that solution 100 percent.

4. Agree on a time in the future to meet and evaluate your progress.

This will be a time to make any necessary adjustments that will be helpful. Without this step of evaluating your progress, all your hard work up to this point will be lost. What if your solution was good but needed a few adjustments that were never made? What if your solution just did not work at all, and you needed to go back to step three again? If you don't evaluate, a few weeks and even months can go by and you'll find that you have slipped back into old patterns. Your lack of follow-through can complicate the problem even more, so take the time to evaluate your progress.

5. Celebrate your success!

This is the fun part so don't leave it out. You have gone through steps one through four by praying and setting aside a time and place to meet, by agreeing on the problem and both of you taking responsibility, by brainstorming possible solutions and choosing one to implement, and by setting a future time to evaluate progress.

Now it is time to celebrate, and there is something special about celebrating our successes. It gives us a sense of accomplishment and also gives us the confidence that no matter what we face, with God's help, there is always a solution. That is truly something to celebrate.

Time-Out

By the third or fourth session, I had a pretty good picture of Charles and Donna and their marriage. Fifteen years of doing things the wrong way takes a toll on people and marriages. It amazes me how easy it is for us to stay stuck in destructive patterns even though they get us nowhere. One of the issues that continued to cause problems for Charles and Donna was how quickly their arguments could escalate. Charles said they could go from zero to sixty in record time, and once they were at sixty, things went from bad to worse in a split second.

So I introduced them to a new tool to put in their marriage toolbox: the time-out.

In almost every sport I can think of, there are time-outs. In baseball, it may be the time a coach takes to assess if his pitcher can continue or needs to come out of the game. In football, it may be taken to design a play for a needed first down or game-winning touchdown. In basketball, the coach may be trying to settle down his players or change momentum. Time-outs are essential in sports, and when and how they are used can play a big role in the success or failure of a team.

> ### What about taking the time-out into your marriage?
>
> Use it just like a coach uses it. Take the time to settle things down, assess the situation, and make adjustments that will ensure a successful outcome.

I suggested the time-out to Charles and Donna and gave them some parameters in how to effectively use it.

First, I told them, just like in sports, the timing of when to use the time-out is important. If you use it simply to stop an escalating fight but do not address the problem, it is wasted. The problem will likely come back with a vengeance.

Second, either spouse has the right to call time-out if they feel things are getting out of hand. The other needs to always honor the time-out.

And third, whoever first called the time-out is responsible for leading the conflict resolution. This means setting the length of the time-out (no more than twenty-four hours) and the place where they would reconvene. During the time-out, both are to spend time problem solving. This means taking time to pray and to think through the steps necessary to resolve the issue when coming back together. The time-out allows a couple to cool down, regroup, and come back together with a new perspective and the goal of solving the problem together.

Donna and Charles bought into the time-out completely. Partly because they were desperate to stop the bleeding and partly because it gave them some hope that even after fifteen years of turbulence, things just might be different.

Would the time-out help your marriage? Could you agree to the same simple steps that Donna and Charles agreed to? The time-out is meant to be a game-changer for a marriage. It was for Donna and Charles, and it can be for you. Let it help you stop the destructive pattern, take time to regroup, and come back with a new focus and purpose.

Preempt Fighting by Connecting

With most couples, the issues that are presented in session one are drastically different from the issues we deal with in later sessions. Often couples just do not want to lay out all the dirty laundry on day one. They may be cautious and need to gain some sense of trust in me. I get that and am completely on board with it. If a couple does not build trust in me, I cannot even begin to help them. Other couples simply are not aware of all the issues that are causing them problems. It takes some time to peel things back and look below the surface.

Whatever the reason, most relationships, especially those that have been unhealthy a long time, are not quickly fixed. It is a process to help a couple work through that which had been stalling growth. When Donna and Charles came to me, the depth of their problems was not readily apparent. Continued counseling eventually revealed a myriad of hidden issues. Their marriage was like walking through a minefield made up of the repercussions of earlier decisions. No wonder they were stressed! Yet as I got to know them better, I saw stress in almost every aspect of their lives.

Donna's job was fast-paced and corporate, and she was one of the stars. Beginning before getting married, she had climbed up the ladder rather quickly and enjoyed the climb.

At the same time, Charles had a very demanding practice. A CPA who owned his own firm, he had an impeccable reputation, and his business grew faster than he ever expected. Charles prided himself on his personal contact with his clients, so he met them for breakfast, coffee, lunch, dinner, drinks; whatever and whenever worked. Golf was also a big part of Charles's life, and he justified the time on the golf course by playing only with clients. Returning tit for tat, since Charles had his golf, Donna decided to take up tennis, playing three evenings a week.

Before marriage, they had talked about having a family, but Donna soon realized she was facing the realities of infertility. Their demanding career commitments caused them to keep putting the tests and procedures off. And now? They would never dream of bringing a child into this mess.

As they recounted their lives, I finally asked them, "When did you have time for your marriage?" The answer was as obvious as their blank stares.

Few couples survive with that level of stress for fifteen years. Without intervention, there will be a breaking point. In the culture of busyness we live in today, it is not unusual for a young couple to try to do too much and put the marriage on the back burner. You cannot begin a marriage, climb the corporate ladder, start a family, fix up a house or two, and expect to build a healthy marriage all at the same time without some level of personal cost.

There are not enough hours in the day, days in a week, or weeks in a year.

You are going to have to make many choices. If you think you can put off building your marriage until later, you will fail. It will not work that way. Remember, God first and spouse second, and all that other stuff we have been talking about in this section has to come behind them.

The Stuff You Don't Have to Fight Over

With Donna's and Charles's career success, you would think they did not have financial issues, but they did. Remember they were on a fast track to success, and they bought into most of the things that go along with that race. New homes, new cars, a boat and lake house (used twice in the past three years), a country club membership, and more. They were never overextended, but they were stretched pretty thin, and that kept them in the race.

As long as they stayed in the race, Donna and Charles looked like they could keep juggling all the balls; but if something went wrong in their careers, everything could come falling down.

As we talked, I asked them to think of the time in their marriage when they were most content. They both came up with the same answer—and curiously enough, it had nothing to do with a lake house or the country club.

For all of Donna and Charles's disagreements, they were in perfect agreement on one thing: They were never more in love than they were before all their stuff entered their lives. Their best days of marriage went back to the early days when the career ladder was in front of them and the climb had yet to begin. The days before big houses, fancy cars, and all the other stuff that we all let our culture tell us screams success. Donna and Charles made a choice in those early days. They could either build a marriage or build an empire. They chose the empire, not realizing they were choosing one over the other.

I recently did an experiment that I think illustrates our ongoing problem with our stuff. As we watched the Super Bowl—and its abundance of commercials—this year, I took a sheet of paper and drew a line down the middle. On one side I listed the commercials that touted products that I needed. These were the products that I honestly could not live without. The other side of the paper was for the "frill" products—products I would like to have but were not necessities. I knew by halftime where my list was going. If it was a boat, it would have capsized—my list was that unbalanced. In fact, all the items were on one side. There was not a single product under my need-this-to-survive title.

My list made me realize there are a lot of things in my life that I want but do not need. I cannot throw stones at anybody who chooses to build an empire. We all have one. Mine may look different from yours, and yours may look different from Charles and Donna's, but if you look you will see one. Neither am I against anyone having nice cars or homes or shoes. But I am against anything that we choose to put above God and our spouse, and if we are not totally honest with ourselves, we can fall into the trap of justifying just about anything we choose to do.

How we see our stuff, and how much we spend on it, is often a hidden issue in marriage that can harm us if we don't take a critical look. We seem to think if someone can pay the bills, they can afford their lifestyle. But paying the bills does not make a good marriage. A great house does not make a good marriage. What makes a good marriage is not what you invest in your stuff, but what you invest in each other.

How do money and possessions affect your marriage? Where are you and your spouse on this issue? Every couple, whether they realize it or not, is trying to build something. The question then is what are you trying to build?

Right and Wrong Influences

If you are in the position Charles and Donna found themselves, how did you get there? Who do you think influenced you? When I asked them that question, they said no one. In fact, I think Charles was a little offended at the question. I knew this was going to take some peeling back to get them to see a bigger picture.

Donna had little time for small talk at work. She was one of those at the top of the company, and it was an all-business-and-no-play corporation. Her main reason for playing tennis, at least in the beginning, was to get even with Charles for the time he spent on the golf course. That response came out of Donna's mouth rather easily. The more she played tennis, the more she liked it, and she was beginning to have something that had been missing from her life for a long time. Friends. The tennis was competitive and intense, but the drink or two after was nice, and everyone seemed to let their guard down.

In the early days it was play tennis, have a drink together, and then get home. As time wore on, the one drink turned into two or three or maybe even four. As their after-tennis time together stretched from thirty minutes to as much as two hours, so did the conversations. As the drinks kept coming, so did the revelations until they all knew each other's secrets.

At first, Donna found some comfort in finding out everyone else's marriage stunk just like hers did. None of her friends cared about improving their marriages, and a couple of the women were even flirting with other men. Nobody encouraged Donna to stick it out in her marriage. No one said there was hope, and no one encouraged her to stop drinking and to go home to spend time with her husband. These women became Donna's closest friends and confidants, yet no one cared that her marriage was falling apart.

Charles, on the other hand, was highly influenced by his family. He was close to his mother, and he had a close older sister who was like a second mom to him. His dad was great but was quiet and kept to himself. His sister had never been crazy about Donna or his marriage. She thought Donna was okay but also thought Donna was not the kind of woman that Charles needed to marry. His mother felt the same way. Over the years they missed few opportunities to voice their opinion about Donna or what Donna did or did not do. It was not an all-out assault, but over time they continued to chip away at Charles and his view of his marriage.

Charles never participated much in these conversations, but he heard every word his mother and sister said and hid them in his heart. It made it easy to make work his focus whether he was in the office, having lunch or dinner with a client, or on the golf course. This was his life, and he rather liked it that way.

As Charles heard Donna tell her story and Donna heard Charles tell his story, the picture came into focus for both of them. They both realized that their view of their marriage was definitely influenced by family and friends, and the influence was not healthy at all for their marriage.

Who influences you?

We all have people who speak into our lives. Some speak health and encouragement and others speak rot and decay. Who do you listen to? Do you listen to those who champion marriage and encourage you as a spouse? Will they commit to help you to stick it out and never give up on your marriage? Do you talk to people who give you hope?

Like it or not, believe it or not, we are influenced by family and friends. If your group of family and friends play the role in your life that they did in Donna and Charles's life, something needs to change. The health of your marriage depends on it.

Conflict Build-Up

When you don't communicate for fifteen years, a lot of important things go unsaid. But it was time for Donna and Charles to play a serious game of catch-up. So I gave them a homework assignment. They were to each make a list of all the expectations they remember bringing into marriage as newlyweds. Then I asked them to each make a second list of their expectations for each other and their marriage today.

Charles's first list was not long and contained no real surprises. He wanted a lot of sex and a wife that took care of him. Taking care of him meant running everything in their lives but his business and running it the way Charles wanted it run. He looked at his list as two simple tasks that Donna had failed miserably to meet. He admitted the sex was good at first but, in his opinion, began to level off pretty quickly. Donna did take care of him, but she did it her way and not his, and that caused a lot of resentment.

Donna's list included romance that would never fade, a husband who provided for her, and a marriage that would grow stronger each year. Strike one, strike two, and strike three. Charles did provide, but she never trusted him to do that at the level she wanted.

Now, can you believe that this was the first time Donna and Charles had ever shared their marriage expectations with each other? Talk about a communication crisis. Fifteen years down the road of life together, and they were each still holding tight to their list of expectations from day one that neither one knew anything about.

The fact that neither Donna nor Charles could write down one current expectation for their life together spoke volumes to all three of us. When you have no hope, you have no expectations. There is no prospect of improvement. Apply this to a marriage, and it is dead and waiting to be buried. Donna and Charles's marriage was in a casket in the back of a limo on the way to the cemetery. The resurrection of this marriage was going to take a miracle.

But it never had to be this way.

What are your expectations in marriage? What are your expectations of your spouse? Does your spouse know what they are? Take time to make your list. Then share your lists with each other. You can now decide if they are realistic or unrealistic. Talk about ways to meet each other's expectations. This process can get you working together in your marriage and seeking to meet each other's healthy, spoken expectations. Your marriage will be better for it.

The Dangerous Waters of Addiction

Addictions are difficult for most of us to understand and even more so when they occur in our marriages. My experience has been that, in most situations, the addiction rules. It comes before spouse, kids, and everything else. Addictions in marriage are the root cause of a lot of the conflict that occurs.

Dysfunction and conflict often go hand in hand. So when we think of addictions, most of us think first of alcohol. It usually gets the most publicity, and AA groups have been a part of our culture for a long time.

Was Donna an alcoholic? It is not my field of expertise, but I do know that she drank to escape, and her times of drinking were detrimental both to Donna and her marriage. It was easy for Charles to condemn Donna for her drinking and to place the blame of a bad marriage on her shoulders. Donna and that group of women she was drinking with ruined his marriage, or so he wanted to believe. I went through a list of other addictions that people deal with in our society today: prescription drugs, street drugs, gambling, sex, porn, computers, exercise, and work.

Work. That was Charles. He was a workaholic. Most of his waking hours centered around his work. He was either in the office or spending time with clients elsewhere. They loved him, and he loved being loved, resulting in Charles becoming addicted to his work.

Go back to our original formula: God first and spouse second. Anything that comes first or second besides those two will cause problems. Most of us can agree on the hazards of excessive alcohol use or drug abuse (prescription or street) or sex or porn. But we often can hide behind work or exercise or ministry because they can make us look and feel good about ourselves.

Therein lies the problem. At what expense do we embrace these? If I have a thriving ministry and people think I am the best marriage counselor ever, but my wife knows I stink at being a husband because I put all my effort into ministry, I have my priorities out of order. This is a trap many of us fall into. Our addictions are "acceptable" in our society because there is an upside to them. My ministry helps people. My company helps the community. My exercise keeps me healthy. There is truth in all of these statements, but where do we cross the line and elevate one of those above our spouse or above God?

Admitting to an addiction is not easy. Every addiction has a payoff. For some it is getting high. For others there is a high not induced by a substance, like others feeding our ego. Often we do not realize when we cross that line, but once we cross it, the return trip can be difficult. Is this section touching a nerve in you? Are you flirting with an addiction? Is something besides God and your spouse slipping into first or second place?

You can do something about it tomorrow or you can do something about it today. Just remember, tomorrow may be too late. Today may not.

The Cost of Not Fighting Right

If this were a novel, at this point in the story Donna or Charles or both of them would realize the error of their ways and fall on their knees before each other asking for forgiveness. Committing to a future life of change, they might renew their vows and live happily ever after. That could be true if this were a novel. This is not a novel.

Charles and Donna divorced. Divorce always saddens me, and this divorce hit me a little harder. I liked them both and I had hope for them. In the end, my hope was not enough; they needed that miracle that never came. Don't get me wrong here. I think the miracle was there for the taking. God was doing His part, but Donna and Charles were stuck.

For Donna it was complex. She knew that to trust Charles again was going to be a big hurdle for her. It was going to be a mountain to climb, and the mountain to her looked like Mt. Everest. This man poured everything he had into everyone but her. All his strokes in life seemed to come from others, and she could not see herself ever being in that place. Besides, she did not need Charles anymore. She was at the top of her career. She had her friends. She was not yet forty, and she saw a brighter future ahead of her. She was sure there was someone better out there for her when she had the time to look around. Donna was done.

Charles, I suspected, stayed in the marriage because he simply did not want to be alone. Basically the only time he was with Donna was when they were both in bed asleep. The other hours of the day were filled with doing what he wanted to do, and Donna seldom crossed his mind. His mother and sister waited for this day. They told Charles how sorry they were, but inside they were so glad to be rid of that woman. They would take care of Charles just like they did before Donna came into his life. They told him things would be fine, and Charles believed them.

In the end, both Donna and Charles wanted out. Both wanted a clean break. They wanted to divide everything up between them, make a few adjustments to balance things out, file for divorce, wait for a judge to sign off on it, and go their separate ways. The hearse pulled into the cemetery. This dead marriage was about to be buried.

Your Turn

Some of you are thinking that your story mirrors Charles and Donna's in many ways. Others are thinking that you could be headed down that same path unless things change. The rest of you may be thinking that could never be us, could it? I do not want you to be the next Charles and Donna. This world already has too many who have given up.

There are all kinds of marriages, but no matter what, I can promise you this: You are going to fight. I have never met a couple who agreed on everything. You will have differences, and differences can bring conflict.

Here's another promise:

You will fight right or fight wrong. If you learn to fight right, good things happen. If you continue to fight wrong, you'll start down a road that you don't want to follow to the end.

Here are some things to consider as you evaluate your fighting patterns. What words do you use? Are they words that bring a positive or negative response from your spouse? Are they healing or hurtful? Are they used to win the battle or to facilitate reconciliation?

When things are going well, talk together about some ground rules to use during conflict. Agree to speak to each other with respect. Do not yell at each other. Listen to each other. Honor the time-out. Set ground rules that lay the foundation for successfully resolving conflict.

Donna and Charles fought wrong for fifteen years. That was not going to stabilize a marriage. If I made a checklist of all the things to do wrong in a marriage and checked all that applied to Charles and Donna, they would have scored one hundred. They were both stressed, and stuff was way too important to each of them. They were negatively influenced by others and flirting with addictions. With expectations that were out of whack, they had lost hope. But neither was committed to making significant changes to turn things around.

Fighting right is not easy. In fact, it takes more time and energy than fighting wrong. We talked about a couple of great tools in "A New Fight Strategy"[1] to help you in the process, five steps to a solution and the time-out. Employing these will give you an opportunity to change destructive patterns, but before using either of those, you have to let God change your heart. Look at your spouse through God's eyes. Remember those hopes and dreams He planted in your heart at the beginning of your relationship with your spouse. Flush out all the lies and focus on His truth about you, your spouse, and your marriage.

Yes, Donna and Charles needed a miracle and so may you, but I believe our God is truly a God of miracles. He is just waiting for you to say, "Come in. We need You. We cannot do it without You." Then link your arms together in His and hang on because a miracle is about to happen!

---

1. Pages 99–103.

BALANCE

Scheduling for a Better Marriage

We learn pretty quickly in this life that part of being human is learning how to balance. We have to learn about balance as we begin to walk, as we learn to ride a bike, and as we play sports. And we learn quickly because if we don't, we'll fall, and though falls can bring pain they can teach at the same time.

Some of our biggest challenges with balance occur in marriage. If all we had to worry about was our marriage, there would not be a problem. But that is not the case. We have work, kids, volunteer work, house work, carpool, church, and all kinds of other things that compete for our time.

Balance in a marriage requires two people. It is only achieved if both a husband and a wife pursue it together. That is the common thread. A marriage gets out of balance when something comes between the two.

Think of a balance scale. You are on one side and your spouse on the other. When you are each doing your part in the marriage, you are in balance. Your focus is on each other and in daily living out God's plan for you as a husband and a wife. This is the way it is supposed to be. Nancy and I have learned a lot about balance as we have lived through our marriage. As I look back at the roughest times, we were out of balance, and as I look back at the best times, we were in balance. It seems so simple looking back.

Staying in balance is like everything else that makes a marriage worthwhile — it takes a lot of work, but just like learning to ride a bike with no hands, the rewards are fulfilling.

If staying in balance is important, don't you think being aware when you are out of balance is equally important? Losing focus on balance is something that took Keith and Katherine by surprise. Keith was a good guy, but his life was out of balance. It was not always that way. There was a time when he was running strong on all cylinders.

The first five years of marriage to Katherine were awesome. Keith was a high school teacher and a football coach. He was not going to get rich at that job, but he loved it and the kids loved him. Katherine was also a teacher and taught in the elementary close to the high school. They had the same vacations and the same days off. Their schedules reeked of balance. There was plenty of time for work, play, and each other. Married life was just like they imagined it would be.

Now you might expect to hear they begin a family and have three kids in three years. But they did not. Or maybe you'd think this is when Keith is promoted to athletic director and his work schedule changes drastically. No promotion. Their schedule remained the same, but their marriage was taking a slow turn for the worse.

What happened is the most common and probably one of the most dangerous things that threaten a marriage because nobody even notices it creeping up. Have an affair and the fingers have a place to point. Start drinking too much too often and things begin to unravel. Come home at the same time every day and spend the same amount of time together as a couple that you always have and no red flags pop up.

By now you are probably either confused or saying "That's us." This is what I think happened with Keith: his life was so balanced that he forgot to be intentional. As a result, he lost his focus and neglected to actively cultivate his marriage.

In the first years of marriage, work was happy and Katherine was happy. Yet ever so slowly, his focus on Katherine blurred. He had the balance—but he didn't work to maintain it.

For example, they used to sit across from each other at their kitchen table and talk for hours. Sometimes they forgot to eat. Now they sat across the room from each other with the TV on till one of them fell asleep. When football season was over in past years, they planned overnight trips on the weekends. They visited every bed and breakfast inn in the state. Now their weekends were like their evenings and, other than church on Sunday, they seldom left the house. Keith spent more time thinking about work and football than he did about Katherine. His time was still balanced, but his focus was not.

The flame was gone in the marriage, and Keith had no idea who had blown it out.

If you're wondering if what happened to Keith is happening to you, try this. Grab a piece of paper and create a pie chart representing your ideal, balanced day.

Let's take my life, for an example. If I divide up my life into portions, it would have God, Nancy, family, work, hobbies, exercise, recreation, sleep, and down time. Let's let my pie chart represent a twenty-four-hour workday. Sleep takes seven and a half hours if I can get it. Work takes about ten hours. God gets thirty minutes. Exercise gets ninety minutes. Hobbies usually get pushed to the weekend. Today, family gets thirty minutes. That was way different when our kids were growing up and at home. I like to have at least an hour of down time each day. That totals twenty-one hours. That gives me three for Nancy.

Twelve percent of my pie chart is available for my wife. Does she get that three hours a day? What do you think? Usually the answer is no.

There is another section of my pie chart that we can label miscellaneous. This covers a lot, and these are the things that daily eat into my time with Nancy. These are the things that can get me out of balance. They usually are not bad things but just things that take time.

Now draw a second pie chart—not of your ideal day, but your real day.

This is where our perfect pie charts are outed as unrealistic. If we're honest, our pie chart of how we'd *like* to use our time looks very, very different from our pie chart of how we *actually* use our time. But here's the real question: What can you change in chart two to bring it more in line with chart one? In other words, as you compare the two charts, how do you bring balance to your life and your marriage?

Let's say you take this whole pie chart thing to heart and rearrange your life to focus on what is most important to you. Since this is a book about improving your marriage, I am going to take a bold step and say you rearranged things to give your spouse more time. That on the surface is a good thing. You are now going to spend more time with your spouse. That will fix your marriage. End of book.

If your quantity of time each day with your spouse is five minutes, make it the most quality five minutes possible. That means talk, touch, and listen.

Not so fast. What about Keith and Katherine? They spent all their free time together, and the marriage was falling apart. Time itself will not solve the problem. The answer is both quantity *and* quality time. If Keith and Katherine kept up the quality of their time together instead of merely existing in the same room, they would be building an awesome marriage.

Balance in a marriage is both about the amount of time a couple spends together and about the way they use that time together. You could spend twenty-four hours a day together as a couple and have a crummy marriage. What a waste of time. Let's look at it this way. How much time do you have for your spouse each day? I will take whatever you have. If it is fifteen minutes, I will take it. If it is more, I will take it.

This is the key. Don't miss this. If your quantity of time each day with your spouse is five minutes, make it the most quality five minutes possible. That means talk, touch, and listen. Look each other in the eye. Sit close together. Laugh. Cry. Be real with each other. Don't be a Keith.

Now let's go back to the pie chart and how it can be deceiving. Keith's pie chart looked pretty good. Lots of hours with Katherine but little quality. What about the couple who carved out only fifteen minutes a day for each other but in those fifteen minutes hit home runs? They cherish that fifteen minutes a day together. They do not let anything get in the way of those fifteen minutes. On their pie chart you can barely see the fifteen-minute slice, but in their marriage you see it written all over each of them. Their fifteen minutes a day gives them balance.

Balance Through Friendship

Balance is a constant battle to maintain, but when you consider the alternative, it becomes more than worth it.

We knew we wanted and needed balance in our marriage. At times it was a struggle. Sometimes I thought we would never achieve the balance we so badly wanted. Yet as time passed, we began to see that balance could become a reality for us. Nancy and I were gaining confidence that our marriage was going to make it. We knew we were not there yet, but we were both headed in the same direction, and it seemed to be the right direction.

We were talking one night, and I asked Nancy a question I had never asked her before: "When things were so bad and the future did not look like things would improve, why did you stay?"

Her answer was simple but spoke volumes to me: "I did not want to lose my best friend."

I was her best friend. I was the one she went to when she was upset, or when she needed a shoulder to cry on, or someone to just listen. No one knew her better than I did because she had never before in her life trusted someone at the level she trusted me.

I guess I knew all those things to be true, but they got lost for me somewhere on the battlefield.

Looking back to the early days of our relationship, we were laying the groundwork for a friendship. We found time to be together, despite the demands of college. We talked about everything, but it was more than just talking; we listened well to each other. I never dated a girl whom I was totally comfortable with until Nancy. Nancy understood me when I did not understand me. I think the reverse was also true. God planted something in our relationship early that has carried us through to today. We were and are each other's best friend.

That fact alone brought an incredible balance to our life together. When we were thinking way too seriously about divorce, I was consumed with fear every time I thought of losing her. Who would I talk to? Who would listen like she listened? Who would understand me like Nancy understood me? The fear came because I never could come up with an answer to any of those questions that made sense to me. Losing her would tip my life out of balance in a way I did not think I would ever recover from.

In a marriage a spouse can fill many roles. All the roles that Nancy fills make my life better. The roles I fill for her make her life better. If all of her roles in my life were lined up side by side and I could pick only one to be fulfilled for the remainder of my life, what would I choose? I admit the choice would be difficult at first, but as I have thought it through, I would pick "best friend." My second choice would be romance. Romance adds a spark, but the problem with romance is that the spark can fizzle and even burn out.

Being best friends gave us a commitment to each other and to our marriage, to stick it out. Being best friends has brought us to our senses many times. If we were in a fight, that element of friendship always helped us calm down. If we said unkind things to each other, our friendship was behind the "I'm sorry." If I could not understand at all why she was doing something, our friendship helped me to be okay without understanding.

When I talk to couples preparing for marriage, I stress the importance of being best friends. Most of them think they are, and I am sure some of them are right. But I encourage them all the same to do some soul-searching. We get married for a number of reasons and "to spend the rest of my life with my best friend" is not always one of them.

Look at it this way. If a couple enters marriage without a strong friendship, I believe marriage will devour them. No matter how great the sex is, without a friendship, it will not sustain a marriage. No matter how much money he or she has, without a friendship the marriage can be empty and hollow. Friendship enables a healthy marriage to grow. I believe that it was this foundation of being best friends that saved our marriage just when it was at its worst.

Who is your best friend? If you are married and your answer is not your spouse—stop everything. You have a job to do. It is not too late. Your spouse needs to be your best friend. Do not let anything stand in the way of that happening. Sure, it will take a lot of work, but you have nothing to lose and everything to gain.

Today take your spouse's hand and sit down and tell him (or her) you want to be his best friend and ask him what he needs for you to do to begin that process. Persevere. Don't give up. You are adding balance to your marriage by valuing your best friend and committing to him or her for life.

Balance Through Time Management

The right friendships can only add to the balance in your marriage. The key here is making sure that these friendships are healthy. I have some great friends who influence me for the better. No doubt you do, too. I know God brought them into my life for a purpose. I don't want to miss out on that. Men do not share at deep levels easily with other men, and when God links us up, we have a great opportunity to learn and grow together.

Nancy, likewise, has a lot of friends, and she amazes me at how she stays connected to them. It seems to come so easy for her, but I know it takes a lot of focus. Her life is richer because of the friends she has, and I would not change that for anything.

Then we have a few couple friends whom we love doing life with. We know their kids and they know ours. We have fun together and are there for each other in good times and bad times. My friends, Nancy's friends, and our couple friends add balance to our lives because they remind us that we must prioritize God first and our spouse second above all else.

A couple of weekends ago, we had three nights in a row of commitments with other couples. They were things we wanted to do and couples we loved spending time with. We enjoyed the weekend and had fun with our friends, but we did not get enough alone time. We were out of balance.

In hindsight, the best thing for our marriage would have been to say no to one of the invitations and take a rain check for a later time. That would have given us the balance we needed. I have learned over the years that my home and my time with Nancy are a refuge for me. It revives me and energizes me. That Monday morning I started the new workweek with my tank about half full. The weekend was out of balance, and so was I.

Wendy and Travis were out of balance. I knew that after one counseling session with them. They had been married fourteen years and probably had been out of balance for fourteen years. About two months into marriage, Travis lost his job. They lived in an apartment but could not handle the expenses with only one income. Wendy's parents offered them her old upstairs bedroom in their home. As they reviewed their options, her parents' offer won.

I know couples who have lived with in-laws for a period of time and had it work out rather well. This living with in-laws did not. Wendy and Travis had no idea how to set boundaries with her parents—who had no concept of boundaries themselves—and so none were set. Two months into marriage, Wendy and Travis fell out of balance because while they were newlyweds, they had precious little alone time.

They ate every meal with Wendy's parents, for example, and felt judged if they mentioned that they were going to eat a meal away from the house. After all, they were living there because they did not have enough money to eat or live elsewhere. Possibly even worse, Wendy and Travis's bedroom was positioned squarely over her parents' on the floor below. Then Wendy mentioned there was no lock on the door.

Despite all this, they thought they could make it through a few weeks. But eleven months later they reached their limit. Finally, they were able to move.

The wait was long, but Travis had a new job and it had a great upside. They found a little house they fell in love with and worked out a lease purchase agreement. Finally a chance to get balanced. Maybe it was living in her parents' house with a bedroom door that did not lock, but whatever the reason, two months into their new home Wendy was pregnant. This first pregnancy was rough on Wendy, but it turned out that numbers two and three were equally rough. Every time they thought things were going to get in balance, something else happened. Life was running them.

As they sat on my couch, they agreed they were totally unconnected and had no time alone together. When I asked them to take me through a typical week, Travis turned to Wendy and said, "Show him your calendar." She looked at him and then at me, and he said again, "Show him your calendar." Wendy agreed and went out to their minivan to get the calendar.

As out of balanced as this couple appeared, Wendy had a system to keep her organized that was pretty amazing. The calendar was on her portable tablet computer. Each day was marked and so were the hours. Then each family member had a color. Travis was blue, and all his activities were on the calendar in blue. Wendy was red, and all her activities were on the chart in red. The kids were green, yellow, and purple. You probably saw this coming, but there was little white space on the calendar, and there was not one spot where the blue and red were together.

The calendar stayed in the minivan because that was command central for Wendy. She and the kids ate in the minivan, did homework there, and took naps there as they went from one thing on the calendar to another. When there were two colors in the same spot, she called Travis in for reinforcement.

Their lives were not just out of balance; they were out of control. Does any of this sound familiar to you? Depending on your stage of life you may think Wendy and Travis were normal. Their lives are not normal but are very common in our culture today. The good news here is that there were answers for Wendy and Travis, and there are answers for you.

This was the most interesting thing to me. Travis and Wendy knew they needed something in their marriage but had no idea what it was or how to get it. They saw that their lives were busy but considered themselves to be a pretty normal family. Maybe you read this story and think the same thing—maybe you see your family in the same situation. I needed to get their attention, so I began, "Let's say nothing in your lives changes and let's play this out over the next ten years. Your marriage will not make it. Your marriage tank is running on empty now. If you can't keep up at this rate, how will you keep up ten years from now?"

I told them I thought I could help them, but a lot of things were going to need to change. Here is the plan I laid out for them.

- We were going to add two new colors to the calendar. We added orange for them as a couple and we added brown for God—their family calendar was so packed, these were the only two colors in the rainbow left to choose from. Each child was going to be limited to two activities a season and only one could be a sport. (Currently each had three or four. For some of you two is too many, but I had to start somewhere with them.)
- Travis and Wendy were to have a date night every week.
- They were also to have a block of time together each day.
- The family was to go to church together each week.

- Only one dinner a week in the minivan. Family dinners at home were to be the new rule.
- Sunday night was to become family night. Everyone had to be there. They could do pizza, games, or whatever as long as everyone was there and everyone participated.

This plan was a huge change, but that was just the beginning. There were other things that I thought we could add as time went on. The key to this would be both of them being 100 percent behind the changes. If they were not together, they would never weather the anticipated storm from the kids. They said they were in. The next step was to tell the kids, and they agreed to do that later in the evening.

The next week Travis told me the story of the family meeting. It was their first-ever family meeting. At first, the kids were silent, and he thought he had put them into shock, but then as they began to talk he realized they kind of liked the idea. Their oldest said, "It's about time somebody took charge around here." (I know that may have been a little disrespectful, but I was wanting to high-five the kid.)

As you looked at Travis and Wendy you may have thought, "That is my/our life." Our culture tells us that crazy schedules are okay, normal, even signs of status and success. In fact, we can believe that if we have free time something must be wrong. Our schedules get us out of balance.

Make Time for Two Things

Right now close this book and go to your weekly schedule. I just want you to look for two things. Where is time for God, and where is time for your marriage? If you did not agree that those two items were important, you probably would not be reading this book. How much time do they get in your week? If nothing changes in your schedule for the next ten years, where will your relationship with God be, and where will your marriage relationship be? Can you afford to ignore the craziness of your schedule? I don't think so, and hey, I can be in the same boat, too. I need balance, and so do you.

Balance Through Having Fun

Steve and Ann had met on a blind date and had so much fun they simply kept dating until they reached the altar. But that was nine years ago. And they weren't having fun together anymore.

When I asked them why they came to counseling, they said they were not happy and felt they were missing out on marriage. They were not thinking about divorce. They just wanted something more in their marriage. I asked them what they did for fun, and they had no response. So I asked what they had done for fun when they were dating. Ann gave me a half smile and said they partied a lot. Steve agreed and said they were very much into the club scene in those days, but now they had kids and were older, and the club scene was off the table as an option.

We need to have times of fun in our lives; when we do not, our lives again get out of balance. Having fun as a couple is important. I asked them what they tried for fun recently and got blank stares. Steve finally said, "Every time one of us suggests something, the other says no." They were stuck, and I wanted to get them moving. I had a plan and asked them if they would follow through if I shared it with them. They agreed.

I gave each a piece of paper. Their assignment was to write down five things they would like to do together as a couple. As I looked over their lists their creativity amazed me. Then I asked them to cut the paper in strips separating the ideas. I put the strips in two envelopes, marking one Steve and the other Ann.

Each week on Thursday they were to draw a slip of paper from one of the envelopes. The first week they would draw from Ann's and the next week from Steve's. They then would continue to alternate each week. There were only two rules. They both had to agree to do what was on the slip of paper, and no complaining.

Two weeks later, Ann and Steve walked into my office smiling again and crediting me as a genius. The truth was that I had not suggested anything that they had not already tried. I simply added a little accountability.

The first slip drawn from Ann's envelope said "bowling." That was something neither had done since elementary school. They had no idea that people still bowled and were shocked when they arrived at the bowling alley that they had to wait for a lane. While they waited, they sat down and watched the other bowlers and laughed with others who were having fun. They together made a wise decision as they finally got an alley to bowl on. They would not keep score.

Somehow that night they got in touch with something that had been missing in their marriage for a long time.

Steve and Ann handled many things well in their marriage. They parented well together and never fought about finances. Now they were adding the fun piece to the pie and ultimately adding more balance to their marriage.

As you try to regain having fun together in your marriage, be intentional about the activities you choose. Maybe like Steve and Ann, you would do better to avoid competitive activities. Nancy and I know this from experience.

In the early years of our marriage, we both played tennis, and Nancy was a better player than I was. (I've never admitted that before.) We did fine playing doubles together, but when we were on the opposite sides of the net, things did not go well. When you are returning a lob and the thought of slamming it in the direction of your wife even crosses your mind, you know something is wrong.

Remember backgammon? Maybe some of you play it now. In the early years of our marriage the backgammon craze was going strong. I purchased a set so Nancy and I could play together at home. I was excited. Yet while it was a great idea in theory, our competitive natures ensured that would be the first and last game we would play together.

It does not matter what you do for fun, but you need to have fun together. If you have things you enjoy as a couple, make sure you set aside time to do them. If you are looking for new things to try, make lists like Steve and Ann did or find out some things your friends enjoy doing as a couple. Having fun together has been and still is one of the great joys in our marriage. Don't miss out on the fun.

Balance Through Family Tradition

Traditions can add balance to a marriage because they can create memories, knit us together, and remind us of what matters the most. Most of us have family traditions, but why wait to have a family? Create your own traditions as a couple.

For example, Nancy and I have a tradition of sitting together in front of our Christmas tree every year. Our first Christmas being married was different for both of us—it usually is for new couples. We wanted to keep some of the traditions from each of our families, but we also wanted to start new traditions of our own. That first Christmas Eve we had dinner with my family at my aunt and uncle's home. There were so many of us that we could not all sit at the table so we gathered in a circle holding our plates stacked with food on our laps. This way we could all be together.

Late that evening we returned to our little apartment. I remember both of us being tired, but we turned off all the lights in the room and sat together in front of our four-foot, dying Christmas tree. It may have been a pathetic little tree, but we picked it out together, and we were in our home in front of our tree decorated our way. Nancy lit a couple of candles and we sat together for a long time. We did not say much. We just took it all in and wanted time to stand still. We have done the same thing year after year. No matter what we do earlier in the evening on Christmas Eve, we end the day together in front of our tree still wanting time to stand still.

Another tradition that we value is celebrating our anniversary—the very first day we committed to loving each other second only to loving God. So to celebrate that day is to celebrate that sacred balance.

On our first anniversary we returned to the scene of the crime, so to speak. We were back in Houston to celebrate with Nancy's family. That was fun but not my idea of a tradition I wanted to keep repeating. The next year we were home for our anniversary and began the tradition of celebrating just the two of us together. There was a great little restaurant downtown with a reputation not only for great food but also for creating special, memorable times for those celebrating there.

Thus started a string of anniversary dinners out that we cherish. We have always tried to go someplace romantic and special for these dinners and have avoided places that were routine for us. In addition to a romantic dinner, I am a little obsessed with greeting cards, and just not any cards. They have to come with the little round gold seal to secure the envelope flap. My tradition came out of an early anniversary when I could not decide on the right card so I bought them all. Nancy got one in the morning and one at noon and one in the late afternoon and one at bedtime. She thought I had gone nuts, but the anniversary tradition with not just one card, but several, was born.

Every time I talk with a couple that has taken a special trip for the first time in a long time their description always includes the statement, "We cannot believe we were not doing this more often." Getting away together adds to balance. It gives us a chance to reconnect and reframe our marriage.

Nancy and I took some memorable trips in the first years of

our marriage. Then the trips we took for a number of years became family trips. Every summer we joined Nancy's family for a week at the beach. I loved it, and it became a great family tradition. My family had a lake house, and it, too, became a family tradition.

It was not until our twenty-fifth wedding anniversary that we rediscovered what going on a trip for just the two of us was all about. We looked through brochures and talked to a travel agent friend before settling on the Caribbean. We booked the trip and began counting the days. Sometimes we plan trips and the hype far outdoes the trip. Not this time. It was near perfect. The beach and water were beautiful. The hotel was incredible. We checked out from the world and never wanted the week to end.

We learned something on that trip that may help you. Don't wait till your twenty-fifth anniversary to go on a romantic trip for two. Plan and save and make it a tradition. It was a jump-start for our marriage, and our only regret was that someone had not encouraged us to do it sooner. We have been back to that same place and hotel many times now.

Tony and Julia had lots of extended-family traditions but none of their own. Tony was Italian. His family of origin was huge, and traditions were everywhere. Julia grew up on a farm, and her extended family included almost all the other farm families in the county. Her traditions were a blending of all these families' traditions put together. In their marriage, the different traditions just caused conflict. Tony wanted his, and Julia wanted hers. In three years of marriage, they had yet to spend Christmas together. Tony went to his family and Julia to hers, and their families were both okay with it. (Sometimes I wish I could just go hit my head against a wall a few times.)

One of my main goals in counseling is to try to help a couple gradually see the need for change and to let them be a part of the process. But my tactic had nothing to do with "gradual" that day. After hearing their Christmas story, I looked at Tony and Julia and said, "That's crazy." So much for the tactful, gentle approach.

Julia said, "I know." Tony said nothing, but he did not leave. I still had his ear.

I talked to them about all the things I have talked to you about in this book. I laid out God's plan for marriage. I talked about how He wanted us in marriage to leave our past life and together build something new. What they were doing was not honoring God's plan, and they were cheating themselves out of the possibility of having an awesome marriage. I gave them this assignment. It was June, but I wanted them to come up with a plan for the following Christmas that included them being together and starting some of their own traditions.

Two weeks later they returned for their second appointment. Julia was all smiles and Tony was some smiles. As we began the session, Tony laid out their plan. It was simple. As they looked at their options, they realized there was not a compromise that would work. That was the reason they had done Christmas apart the past three years. His family would not budge and neither would hers.

So their solution was to celebrate Christmas alone—just the two of them—and start to establish their own new traditions. They planned to tell their families of their decision in July, thinking the sooner the better. I liked it. It was bold and daring, but not as crazy as what they had been doing. I was leaving for vacation, so we decided to meet the first week of August. Their job was to tell the families and put a little more structure around their own plans. Finally, they were on the same page and working together.

The family, of course, wasn't too happy about their solution. There was pushback, threats, and even a tearful call to Tony from his great-grandmother. Through it all, Tony and Julia stood firm. We met a few more times before Christmas. Both families were sure Tony and Julia would cave in, but they did not.

When we met in January, they shared an interesting effect of their holiday decision. Both families wanted to talk about the next Christmas, and both were willing to compromise. Tony and Julia learned a lot over those six or seven months. They learned about putting their marriage where God wanted it to be. They learned about the importance of having their own traditions, and they learned about the importance of balance.

What about you? What are your traditions? Are there new ones you would like to start? If your traditions are not adding to the balance in your marriage, maybe it is time to reevaluate them and make some changes.

Financial Balance

Danny called my office for an appointment and came in to see me a week later. Danny was married, and a married guy coming to counseling on his own is a rarity. Usually if anyone comes alone, it is the wife; and if both come, usually the wife schedules the appointment. Danny began to tell me why he was there.

They learned about putting their marriage where God wanted it to be, about the importance of having their own traditions, and about the importance of balance.

Jamie was the love of his life. They attended the same high school, but during those years Jamie had no idea that Danny existed. It was a big school with lots of students. Jamie was with the "in" crowd and Danny was with the "out" crowd, but that never stopped Danny from dreaming. They both went out of state to college, and it was the summer after their junior year that they "officially" met. Time and a little maturity had changed things, and Jamie was open to that first date. For Danny, that summer was the best summer of his life as he spent time with Jamie almost every day. By the next summer they were engaged, and they married the following Christmas. Danny could not have been happier.

Things continued to fall into place. They both got good jobs with companies they liked and that provided growth opportunities for each of them. Danny brought in over half of the family income and handled the finances. They both struggled with overspending at times, but their good incomes covered most of the problems. They traveled some and were enjoying marriage.

As the years passed, they began to talk about starting a family and buying a larger home. They both would turn thirty the following year. Looking for homes became a Sunday afternoon ritual. They found things they liked and things they did not like and were narrowing down the list of what they wanted in this new home. Even though they never discussed it, they both knew they were looking at homes that were probably out of their price range.

Then two things happened. Jamie got a big bonus at work and Danny got a raise. Bring on the paperwork—they were buying that house they never thought they could afford. If you have ever bought a new home that was much larger than the home you had been living in, you know that the increased mortgage payment is only part of the increased expenses. They needed more furniture and more stuff, and Danny was discovering all this cost much more than he ever thought it could. He did not panic but had a lot of concerns.

Each time he approached Jamie to discuss it, he was met with an, "It's okay. I will get another bonus in six months and we can pay things off then." The bonus came and bills were paid, but new bills were incurred.

The pattern of buy now and pay in six months became routine. Danny relaxed a little, as things seemed to be working the way Jamie said they would. He did not think they were being the best stewards of what God had blessed them with, but every time he tried to broach the subject with Jamie, he was stonewalled.

For Danny's birthday, Jamie surprised him with a new swimming pool for the backyard. She had all the details worked out with the pool company, and construction would begin the next week. According to Jamie's calculations, they would have it paid off completely with her next two bonus checks. The idea scared Danny at first. After all, it was a huge investment. As the construction began, he relaxed a little and decided he could get into the home-with-a-pool life. The same week they opened the pool, Jamie got her next bonus check. The amount was less than they expected, but Jamie assured Danny the next check would more than make up the difference.

When the check came in, it was less than half of what Jamie led Danny to believe it would be. Now Danny panicked. They had a pool they could not pay for. If it was a car, he would have turned it in or sold it, but you cannot return a pool. It looked like they might be forced to sell their house, and Danny was angry. His anger was at himself and at Jamie. He had never been in debt in his life, and instead of doing what he thought was right, he had given in and now they were in a mess both financially and in their marriage. Their finances were out of balance and their marriage was on the ropes.

Problems with money are consistently one of the main issues that get couples out of balance. Money is the most mentioned topic in the New Testament. That is somewhat reassuring to me. It tells me God is not surprised that we can all struggle with money. We have an interesting dilemma in our culture. Few of us consider ourselves rich, but the rest of the world looks at us and thinks we are rich. Their perspective is different from ours. We get caught up in what we do not have instead of looking at what we have.

A few years ago, a neighbor friend purchased a new, expensive sports car for himself for Christmas. It was beautiful and fast and looked incredible sitting in his driveway. I like cars, but I had never, ever even thought about this make and model until it sat down the street from me. Now I wanted one! Is that warped? The answer is yes—it was warped.

Let's say I played out that obsession and hocked everything I owned and bought a similar car. What would I gain? I would have a car I could not afford. I would have other bills I could not pay and, at best, I would have an unhappy wife. I would have shot my financial balance. Most of you reading this book would be considered rich by the rest of the world's standards. Here is the key to staying rich. Don't miss this. It's not what our culture says to do. It is "live within your means." It's that simple. If you don't have it, don't spend it. Period.

Balance in the financial area of our marriages is essential. According to studies, money is the number one issue couples fight about.[1] In other words, if a couple struggles with money they usually will struggle with their marriage. A balanced checkbook, controlling spending, and setting aside money to save can lead to a balanced marriage. Danny had the right plan for their money, but he gave in to Jamie for all the wrong reasons. In the back of his mind was this fear, "If I say no, she will leave me. I cannot believe I won her heart in the first place."

That is a dangerous position for spouses to find themselves in. Talk about being out of balance in your marriage. That is about as bad as it can get. In a marriage, the role of the husband and the role of the wife are both equally important, and both bring much to the marriage. When one feels less than the other, it diminishes their role and goes against God's plan for their marriage, and bad things begin to happen.

The next week Jamie came in with Danny. Guess what? She was a wife who wanted her marriage to work. I told them while I would work with them on their marriage, I also wanted them to see a financial planner. Today Danny and Jamie are back on track. They made some tough decisions as they sold their home and paid off all their debt.

The next step was probably equally important as they vowed to stay debt free in the future. With the help of the financial planner, they began investing Jamie's bonuses and planned both short- and long-term purchases, paying cash for everything. With the

---

1. XO Group, "New Survey Reveals: Money Number One Cause Of Conflict For Engaged Couples, Newlyweds And New Parents," PR Newswire (August 22, 2012): http://www.prnewswire.com/news-releases/new-survey-reveals-money-number-one-cause-of-conflict-for-engaged-couples-newlyweds-and-new-parents-167025135.html.

financial issues behind them, my job as a marriage counselor was relatively easy. Now they had a new beginning and an unwavering commitment to financial balance.

Your Turn

If I sat down today with you and your spouse and asked you if your marriage was in balance, what would you say? Which of the couples you met in this section could you identify with?

Keith and Katherine had a lot of time together with no connection, and their marriage lost its balance. Remember, it is about both the quantity and the quality of the time you spend together. Travis and Wendy and their three kids were living out of a minivan with a nice home pretty close by. As hard as Wendy tried to make sense of their schedules, they were way out of balance.

Pick one thing that would add balance to your marriage if you began doing it consistently as a couple.

Steve and Ann were settling for a marriage of two people just existing together. The lack of fun together put their marriage out of balance. Tony and Julia were letting the fear of breaking family traditions break their balance. Danny and Jamie made financial decisions that destroy many marriages. Restoring financial balance was the key to restoring their marriage.

Your story may be similar to one of these, or it may be different; but no matter your story, balance takes work.

Let me give you a suggestion.

Pick one thing that would add balance to your marriage if you began doing it consistently as a couple. Now that you have your one thing, where and when do you start? What are your obstacles? How can you together remove them? Don't give up. Keep at it, and you will begin to experience more balance in your marriage.

Secret Number 6:

MINGLE

Sex as the Mingling of Souls

We've talked about conflict, about communication, about balance, and about fighting fair—now let's talk about sex. More importantly, let's talk about what it takes to have the best sex ever. I think the answer will surprise you because you probably will not see it tonight on the late show.

As much as I wanted to know everything there was about sex at age twenty-two and as a newlywed husband, I was sorely lacking. My sex education came from my peers and a poorly done sex education film I saw in sixth grade. Let's just say there were animated cartoon sperm with smiley faces.

My church home tried to help by having a local physician come to spend time with the youth group. The premise was that he would make a few remarks and then we could ask him questions. The youth lounge was packed; he made a few remarks and then opened things up to questions, which was followed by thirty minutes of silence. I felt sorry for the doctor, for the church that tried, and for the teens that went away more frustrated than ever.

As guys, it seems that we think we have to know everything about sex. We think we have to be sex experts. I am not exactly sure where that thought originated, but it seems like it has been passed down from generation to generation for a number of years.

Nancy grew up in Houston, which was south and east and about eight hours away from where I grew up in Oklahoma City, but that didn't seem to make much difference in her sex education, which was less than mine. She didn't even have friends who faked knowing about sex. Probably a male/female thing at that time in our culture. Basically Nancy was taught that sex was wrong and dirty and it would ruin your reputation forever. She was the oldest of three girls, and that was the message given to each of them. It was the prevailing sex education philosophy for girls at that time — and unfortunately, it is still taught today by some. Match that with hormones, and you have mass confusion at best.

By the time we met in college, Nancy was still a virgin, and I was not. This posed a dilemma for me for more than one reason. Around my friends I thought it was cool to boast of my manhood, but around Nancy I wanted to be a virgin again and bring the same thing that she brought to our relationship and hopefully future marriage. We never talked much about my past. At some point in our relationship, she knew I was not a virgin, and she chose to stay around. I never asked for her forgiveness till a few years after our marriage, and it was then that I learned Nancy had already forgiven me years before.

However, what I did and what I counsel others to do are different. If I had a do over in sharing about my past with Nancy, I would take it. Since I do not, this is the counsel I give couples today when asked this question, "Should I share my sexual past with my fiancé?"

My answer is yes and no. The yes is that I believe sharing our past continues to build the relationship of honesty and openness. It is also important for you to know that your future spouse knows all about you and still chooses you. The no comes with the details. It is one thing to share past relationships and the extent of sexual involvement. It is another to give a play by play description of all the details. I have never seen that to be helpful at all.

On the day we married, Nancy was twenty (barely) and I was

twenty-two (also barely). She looked incredible. We did all the traditional things. We did not see each other on our wedding day, and I was not allowed to see her dress until the night she walked down the aisle. She was truly the most beautiful thing I had ever seen. As she reached the front of the church, I had no idea if I could speak or not. Thankfully I was able to repeat my vows and say, "I do." The ceremony for me was just a blur, and we were soon in the backseat of a limo headed to our reception.

Every couple has their own wedding night story. For some it is the fairy tale come true. For others, the skyrocket never quite takes off—at least not right at first. My counsel to couples headed to marriage is to keep the wedding night expectations realistic. If the skyrocket launches, great! If it fizzles, you have many more nights to let that part of your marriage develop. Whatever it is for you, recognize that the wedding night experience is step one in the process of building the sexual relationship you will have for the rest of your lives.

As guys, we are all about the mechanics. We are very intrigued with the way sex between a husband and a wife works—the way our bodies have been designed by God to dance together. Somehow many of us thought our wives were also all about the mechanics. That is the message we have been given many times by our culture. Interestingly enough, God created us more than a little different in this area.

In my counseling practice, I see time and time again that women want romance and trust and commitment and security. If those are in place, then bring on the sex. Men, on the other hand, often believe they are expressing those very things—romance, trust, commitment, security—through sex itself. So how do we learn to understand each other and meet each other's unique needs? To do this, we have to go back to the very beginning.

Sex as a Gift

God gives us a pretty clear picture of His design for sex in the Bible. You may be saying, "Sex in the Bible? No way." You are probably saying that because you think God is some prude up in the sky somewhere.

Allow me to burst your bubble. First, who do you think created sex? Second, who do you think made a man and a woman in a way that they fit together sexually? Third, who put all those sensory nerves that give us pleasure in the man's and the woman's body parts? As difficult as it is for many of us to see sex as another incredible gift from God, it truly is, and God wants us to enjoy it fully as husband and wife.

In the first chapter of Genesis, God shares His plan for procreation, "Be fruitful and multiply." How do you think God meant for us to do that? You know, if He wanted a stork to bring babies, He could have done that, but that is not the way we get babies. Be fruitful and multiply! Then flip over in your Bible to the book named Song of Solomon. In this book you see Solomon make love to his wife two different times. One time he begins at her feet and moves up. Another time, he starts at her head and moves down. He talks about her breasts and of making love to her all night long. Some of you who have never picked up a Bible are now considering doing so. That is encouraging!

The Bible also tells us in Genesis that a man and his wife will become "one flesh." Let me give you my take on this. First, the one-flesh dynamic happens, of course, on a physical level. Though in truth, any man or woman can be joined this way, whether married or single, Christian or non-Christian. My take is that for Christian married couples there is the possibility of experiencing that one-flesh phenomenon uniquely, on an emotional and spiritual level.

The oneness that occurs is indescribable. Why is this true? There are probably a number of reasons, but there are two that I think are very important. First, there is something very special about a Christian married couple receiving God's gift of sex the way He designed it to be received. Second, there is a spiritual dimension for Christian couples that is difficult to describe but adds much to the experience. Does every Christian couple experience this? Probably not, or at least not every time, but the possibility is there for each and every one of them.

There is a word used in the Hebrew language for this experience. The first time I heard it, I was listening to a message on the Song of Solomon by Pastor Matt Chandler of the Village Church. The word is *dod*, and the definition of *dod* is "a mingling of souls." How much closer can two people get? Let me spell it out this way.

When a Christian couple is doing all the things we talked about in steps one through five and are joined together physically making love, this mingling of souls takes place, and that is why I firmly believe that the best sex ever is in the context of a Christian marriage. Why? Because sex in the God-first, spouse-second marriage is about more than mechanics. It has a spiritual element too, making physical oneness all the more deep. There is only one reason to become a Christian, and that is to have a personal relationship with Jesus Christ, but some of the side benefits are amazing. Without a doubt, one of these is *dod*.

God's Plan for Purity

The idea of staying pure until marriage gets lost in the cultural cry when it comes to sex. Our culture insists, "Have sex and have it a lot, and don't even bother thinking about waiting." This part of God's design for marriage is a tough sell. Some of you are already skipping to the next chapter. Let me put it this way. I don't think it is my job here to convince you to choose purity before marriage. My job, as I see it, is to just give you some things to think about. The choice is the same as it always has been — it is yours.

Christopher and Anna were engaged to be married. They were sitting in the front row of the "Preparing for an Awesome Marriage" class I was teaching. Like I did with most of the couples, I soon learned their front story. They shared their wedding date and plans along with the details of where they worked and how they met. It was later that I learned their backstory.

Christopher was twenty-seven, and this would be his first marriage. He came close a couple of times but never made it all the way to the altar. He was sexually active in high school, college, and after, including his two serious relationships. Anna had made the decision to save herself for marriage, but a long-term relationship in college changed all that. Since college, there were two other guys who ended up as serious relationships. By their mid-twenties, neither was satisfied with the direction their lives were headed, and each decided to try a different path. Christopher's best friend was attending a new church that he liked. The next Sunday, Christopher tagged along and felt right at home. This might be what he was looking for.

At the same time, Anna was actively looking for a church to call home. Two Sundays later, she walked into that same church Christopher was attending.

The church was different from anything either of them had experienced in the past. The pastor was culturally attuned and had a way of teaching from the Bible that was relevant and made sense. Even though the church was fairly new, there were almost a thousand people there on Sunday mornings. At this point in their lives, neither Christopher nor Anna was looking for a relationship, but the Sunday they just happened to sit down side by side stirred something in them both. "Who is this guy?" and "Who is this girl?" and "How did we end up sitting together?" Little was said by either of them as the service ended other than the obligatory pleasantries. The following Sunday, Christopher was on the lookout for Anna and somehow sat by her again. This time they talked, and a relationship began.

> I have never talked to a person or a couple who chose purity and regretted it, nor to a person or a couple who chose to be sexually active outside of marriage and said they were completely fulfilled.

I love how God works. Both Christopher and Anna were considering making a renewed commitment to purity before marriage. It was more of wanting to try it God's way, since their way had not worked out, than a deep conviction in either of them. The deep conviction of doing it God's way came later as they made the commitment together to keep their relationship pure.

It would be nice if I told you that the commitment was the hard part and the rest was easy, but that was not what happened. In fact, it was just the opposite. The verbal commitment was easy, and then almost every day was a struggle. The doubts flooded their minds. "Was this what we were supposed to do?" "Wasn't the Bible written for people a long time ago?" "Could God really expect us to stay pure till marriage in this day and time?" The answer to each question was always yes. Their dating and engagement period lasted almost two years, and finally the day of their wedding came. They made it. This relationship was pure.

Three months into their marriage I sat down with Christopher and Anna. We talked about many things before I finally asked them this question: "Was the waiting worth it?" Without a pause, both answered, "Yes." This is the essence of what I heard them say. God totally redefined sex for them. What they were experiencing was different from anything they had ever experienced in the past. Before, they had no idea what *dod* was all about. Today they were living it.

What I want you to hear is that we serve a God who redeems our past. Whatever sexual choices you made in the past are just that. They are in the past. Today is a new day, and the God of the universe wants to redefine your life. Would you be willing to take a chance on this? I have never talked to a person or a couple who chose purity and regretted it. I have never talked to a person or a couple who chose to be sexually active outside of marriage and said they were completely fulfilled. Once again, you have a choice. What will you choose?

On Sexual Differences

If God had made men and women both with male sex drives, what would that look like? If God had made men and women both with female sex drives, what would that look like? The solution is, of course, that He did not, and this is both good and bad news for us all. Because we are different, it adds to the fun; but because we are different, we have to learn what makes the other one tick. Let's start with men.

Most men think about sex more than their wives. Most men want to have sex more times a week than their wives. Most men fantasize about sex with their wives. Yes, these are generalities, and yes, there are always exceptions to generalities, but again and again, this is the trend that comes out in the counseling office. If you are a wife and your sex drive is sometimes or always stronger than your husband's, of course, there is absolutely nothing wrong with you. I have counseled many couples where this was true. But for many men, the greatest satisfaction in the sexual relationship in marriage is knowing that he can bring his wife pleasure and that she is drawn closer to him because of their sexual relationship. Now that, to him, is romantic.

The myth is that a man could have sex with the house burning down around him. While there is an element of truth in that statement, the real truth is that a husband does not just want a body to perform on. He wants a responsive wife who also gets pleasure out of the sexual relationship with him.

A wife's list of what she wants in the sexual relationship in marriage is exactly the same as her husband's list.

I'm kidding. I just had to say that. The sexual desires of a wife, as you well know, are very different from those of her husband. Let me help you with this, guys. Your wife's needs will probably never make sense to you, but they do not have to make sense. You just need to accept the fact that her wiring is very different from your wiring. That way you do not spend a lifetime trying to change her or figure the whole thing out.

She needs to be able to trust you. It is more than trusting you to be faithful to her, even though that is essential. It is knowing that you will never lie to her or knowingly hurt her. It is knowing that you will never neglect her all day only to use her at night, but rather, that you will love her all day and love her in bed just the same. It is trusting that in the sexual relationship you will not take advantage of her in any way. It is knowing that when she is at her most vulnerable in your arms, she is also at her safest. Don't ever violate that trust. Stay at her comfort level.

She needs to know you will be faithful to the commitment you made to her before God on your wedding day. That commitment was for life, made in a culture that counts commitment in minutes. There is only one way to show this lifetime of commitment, and that is simply being there every day for the rest of your life. That is what she wants and what you both need, but real commitment takes it a step further.

Real commitment is being immersed in the marriage. It goes much deeper than your daily presence. Look at it this way. I can live out fifty or so years of marriage and never be unfaithful and always be around but never invest in my marriage. I can say I am committed but never really give of myself. As much as I hate what divorce does to lives, I almost hate as much what happens when couples just exist together. They eat at the same table, sleep in the same bed, sit side by side in matching recliners as they watch TV, and have no clue what is going on inside each other. To me, that is not a marriage. That is coexisting—not exactly the picture of romance, and certainly not what God had in mind.

Our world is way too full of couples who go through the motions of marriage on the outside without being married on the inside. The Bible compares the marriage relationship to Jesus' relationship to the church. That relationship is one of sacrificial love and affection. It is an incredibly close relationship that is connected forever. Commitment is about giving your heart to someone else 100 percent. It takes *commitment* as a noun and turns it into *commit* as a verb. It is an action word both on the outside and the inside. It changes marriages and knocks down the obstacles that can stand between a husband and his wife.

Being faithful to the commitment of a monogamous relationship in marriage is an essential part of God's design for marriage in a world that increasingly sees it as nonessential. Being faithful here means your entire sexual focus is on your spouse and your spouse only. It means laying strict boundaries with the opposite sex and keeping them. It means no porn in any form. I have had many women whose husband is into porn ask me this question: "Why does he look at that when he has me?"

This is a very real question, resulting in very real pain. And it's up to you, men, to avoid causing such pain. God's plan for me sexually in marriage is just that: sex is to be totally contained in my marriage. No porn. No strip clubs. No flirting. No mentally undressing anyone but my wife. My sexual thoughts, ideas, and fantasies center on Nancy and on her alone. I know what some of you are thinking, that what I am saying is countercultural and seemingly old-fashioned, but my answer is simple. From years of talking to couples, this way works, and the world's way does not.

These issues do not lie strictly with men, either. It was not that long ago that all the discussions on porn centered on men and visual porn. Today, more and more women are flirting with porn, mostly in written form. Women's magazines, sexual books, and novels seem to be getting most of the attention. The bottom line is this. Whether you are male or female, you have to ask this question, "Is this God's plan for my marriage?" My firm belief is that God gave us everything we need to have a more than great sexual relationship. The best sex ever is simply a husband and a wife coming together naked and unashamed and totally enjoying together the bodies God gave them.

In general, wives are usually more verbal than their husbands. Certainly, that is not always true; but verbal or not, most wives seem to want some level of good communication with their husband. For a woman, communicating with her husband is that connection cord that links them together. In my opinion, good communication between a husband and a wife is not an option. It is an absolute necessity. Without it, the marriage suffers, and the sexual relationship will never reach its full potential.

Finally, your wife needs you to understand how important nonsexual touching is to her. Many of us guys think that non-sexual touching was that touching we were forced into before marriage because sexual touching was off-limits or supposed to be off-limits. We have two touching categories. Nonsexual before marriage. Sexual in marriage.

It never crosses our minds that nonsexual touching has a place in marriage until our wives somehow address the subject. You may have heard these words, "Do you have to grope me every time you touch me?" or "Can't you just hold me?" or "Does it always have to be about sex?"

Nancy used all these phrases in one way or the other, plus a few more. I did not get the message until I realized she was sleeping as close to the edge of her side of our king-size bed as she could get. There was an ocean of sheet between the two of us. Not only was she far away, but her back was also to me, and she was usually asleep or acting like she was asleep before I ever got in on my side of the bed. This brought me to an amazing conclusion: I needed to listen to what she was saying. I know. I amaze myself at times with the revelations I come up with.

It should not take a dictionary for you to unravel the definition of nonsexual touching. It is self-defined. Nonsexual touching is not touching her sexual parts. Keep your hands off her breasts and rear end and vagina. Nonsexual touching is holding hands, cuddling, putting your arm around her, holding her close, and sitting close together.

I made a deal with Nancy to get her to move closer to my side of the bed. (Some of you are going to hate this idea, but it worked for us and might possibly work for you.) My pledge was that I would only do nonsexual touching unless she initiated or expressed a desire for more. The minute these words left my mouth, I regretted them. What had I done? First, I thought I could never, ever follow through with this, and second, if I did, I would live out the rest of my married life with no sex.

With God's help, neither of these fears came true. And guess what I learned through this process? I learned not only to like but also to value nonsexual touching. Before marriage, it was default touching, and I put it in the category of second best; but now I was choosing it. I was choosing to hold her hand, to embrace her with my hands around her waist, and to keep them there. I was falling asleep in bed while cuddling her and waking up that way in the morning. Did I want sexual touch? Sure. That desire never left, but we were redefining our sexual relationship in a good way.

If Nancy had never made her point about nonsexual touching and if I had never listened to her, we would have missed out on an important part of our marriage. As I honored her, it was not long until our sexual relationship revitalized, but it was different. We had added some important connecting pieces. Do I still struggle at times? Sure. But I have learned there is a time and a place for every kind of touching in marriage, and all of them are good and need to be a part of the sexual relationship. It is about balance, and balance is always good in a marriage.

Now you have a choice. You can continue to believe what Hollywood usually tells us about male and female sex drives, or you can see there are differences. I believe those differences were and are a part of God's plan. We can embrace these differences or reject them. If you reject them, you may quickly find yourself back in insanity land. You are trying again and again to get a different result instead of accepting things as they are. If you embrace them, you are not just making the best of things but seeing what God's best is for you and your marriage.

In a healthy marriage, a husband and a wife have the opportunity to learn from each other. If we were the same, there would be nothing to learn, and honestly, I think we would eventually get bored. By having differences and embracing these differences, we have a chance to grow, experience more of what God has for us in marriage, and build something special.

Men and Sex

What are some of the things that a guy can do to improve his sexual relationship with his wife? Here we go. First, I think we need to figure out how to be romantic. What are your ideas on this? Who are your role models? I was pretty lucky in this area because my dad was good at the whole romance deal. He brought my mom gifts, took her to dinner, played music for her, danced with her, and treated her with great respect. I witnessed all of this growing up, so I started off marriage thinking I was going to hit home run after home run in the romance department.

I did pretty well but needed to make an adjustment. Nancy was not my mom. All the things that I saw work with my mom did not work with Nancy. For me, that was frustrating. As a guy, I wanted a formula that worked that I could repeat over and over for the entire life of our marriage. I never got that, and I don't think most guys get that. If you want to know what she thinks is romantic, ask her. It can get a little sticky here if your wife somehow has bought into the myth that if you really love her you will just know.

The bottom line is that we cannot read each other's minds. Ladies, try this. Just tell him what you think is romantic. Give him credit for asking and following through, and if he does not follow through, you have my permission to get all over him.

Nancy likes gifts but not like my mom liked gifts. My dad could bring my mom a gift, and she lit up like a Christmas tree. It made her feel loved and was the exact same thing her dad did for her and her mom. When I gave Nancy a gift, I knew she liked it; but her reaction was different from what I saw in my mom. Gifts did not affect Nancy the way they did my mom. I was stumped. What would have the effect on Nancy that gifts did on my mom?

In the years that I lived at home, my dad was involved in a lot of organizations and attended a lot of meetings. I never heard my mom complain about this. I have also been involved in a number of different things and early in our marriage could be gone a lot. Nancy complained. She would tell me that she wanted us to have more time together, and it took me a fairly long time to really hear what she was saying. She was asking for more time with me, and when I finally began giving her more time, our marriage relationship took a big step forward.

Just knowing that I made her a priority and that I set aside time each day and week for just the two of us was romantic to her. It made a difference. She needed my time, and I could do that. (Plus it was a lot less expensive than the gifts thing.) I might have eventually figured out on my own what made her feel loved; but I needed Nancy to tell me, and when she did, it was my job to follow through.

Usually the spouse who has the strongest sex drive will do more of the initiating. As we discussed earlier, this is most often, but not always, the husband. As men, we have a tendency to rush the process. The words *instant* and *fast* and *quick* are applied to everything from food to workouts. When we throw the sexual relationship into this rushed lifestyle, we tend to leave out an important part, and that is sexual foreplay. The main problem for our culture with sexual foreplay seems to be that it takes time, and we don't give it the time. Thus we miss out on the things that heighten the senses and prepare us for intercourse.

What do you want to be a part of the sexual foreplay in your marriage? Think about it and then talk about it with each other. Commit to set aside time for sexual foreplay. It is easy to get into sexual ruts, and then the sex can become routine. Don't let that happen to you; and if it has happened, fight back. Fight for a sexual relationship that is amazing and draws you close to each other in all ways possible.

Finally guys, make yourself sexy. Let me put it another way.

Make yourself appealing. Remember when you were dating? Most of us put an effort into our appearance. We cleaned up and thought about what we were going to wear. We wanted to impress her and to be appealing. Why not do the same things in marriage? Do the basics. Bathe. Brush your teeth. Keep yourself fit and take care of your appearance. Wear cologne, and let her pick it out, because she is the one smelling it. I used to pick out the colognes I liked. I think I went for the rustic smell (whatever that is). It was not working, but Nancy always said she wanted me to wear cologne.

Then on an anniversary trip to the Caribbean, things changed. It was a rainy morning, so we gave up the beach and headed to a shopping area. It was there my life changed. We came to a men's fragrance counter, and Nancy began trying different colognes on me. She found one she liked and encouraged me to purchase it. That evening after I showered to prepare for dinner, I sprayed myself with the new cologne. That night was probably the best sex we had experienced in a long time. I wore that cologne the rest of the trip, and our sexual relationship hit new heights. I swore to wear it the rest of my life.

It was probably a month after we returned home that I came to the realization that the Caribbean must have played a part in Nancy's reaction to my cologne, but I did learn a valuable lesson. I don't buy cologne without her, and I let her pick it out.

Women and Sex

Just as there are things a husband can do to improve the sexual relationship in his marriage, there are also things a wife can do. The first seems simple, but it can get complicated. For you as a wife to accept your husband's sexual needs may be a challenge because God made us different. As you are lying in bed thinking about how to improve the communication between the two of you, he may be lying next to you thinking about making love.

Certainly both the husband and the wife can fantasize about their sexual relationship, but most husbands do it more. It is a difference that may never make sense to a wife, but it is a fact of life. Whatever your situation, it is one of those differences to embrace, and if you do not, it can cause a lot of frustration for both of you.

Consider this. Your husband chose *you*. You are the most sexy person he has ever seen. If you are in a healthy marriage, and I pray that you are, his desire is for you and you alone. Cherish that.

There are times even after all these years of marriage that Nancy still looks at me and shakes her head. It might be a time when she thinks she looks her worst, and I tell her she has never looked prettier; or I can think she looks sexy when sex is the furthest thing from her mind. Even though I think she does not understand all this about me, I think she has not only learned to accept it but also to cherish it as something good from someone who loves her. Plus it is a lot easier than dealing with the thought that her husband might really be nuts.

I find in counseling that few couples talk about their sex life. They seldom ask each other what they like or do not like. They don't talk about what they would like to try. That will never move your sex life forward. It is just as important to talk about your sex life in your marriage as other things that you deem important. Sometimes women tell me they are afraid to ask their husbands what they want in their sex life. They are hesitant to hear what he will say. This is what I tell them: "Ask. Let him express himself. If you do not want to do what he suggests, you can always say no—but ask."

Remember that God gave us our bodies to enjoy in the sexual relationship in marriage. There is a lot to explore, and anyone who says their sex life is boring has just gotten lazy or complacent. Don't be afraid of being an explorer with your spouse. You may find an amazing new territory.

Here are some questions to get you started:

- What is the best sexual experience you have had in your marriage?
- What made that time special?
- What do you enjoy the most in foreplay?
- Is there anything you do not like or is uncomfortable for you?
- Is there something you would like to try?
- What time of day is best for you?

It is just as important for a wife to make herself sexy as it is for her husband to do the same for himself. The difference is this. As a wife, if you are breathing, you have probably accomplished this task. It is not complicated. Yet, our culture is hard on women. There is this image of the perfect beautiful woman that no one can live up to.

Ladies, let me share this, and please hear me. This is the way I look at Nancy, and I think it is the way many men look at their wives. I honestly think she is more beautiful today than ever before. What attracted me at twenty is different from what attracts me today. We have grown up together, and I see so much more in her now than just outward beauty. As I am writing this, Nancy just came into my study to give me a kiss as she was leaving for an appointment. As she turned to go, I told her she looked beautiful—and she did, and she does.

What attracted me at twenty is different from what attracts me today. We have grown up together, and I see so much more in her now than just outward beauty.

Believe your husband when he tells you that you are beautiful because he is really the only one who counts. Just don't take your husband for granted. Make the effort to look nice for him and take care of your appearance. Also, just like I suggested to the men, let your husband be a part of picking out your perfume.

What About Distractions?

As I have talked to couples about their sexual relationship over the years, I have realized most of us have the same or similar struggles. When we married, I had incredibly high expectations for our sexual relationship. I guess I thought rockets would go off every time we made love and that we would make love a lot. In theory, that sounded pretty good to me. In reality, it takes work to keep the rockets going off.

In the early years of our marriage, I think most of our sex was hormone driven—and mine did a lot of the driving. If someone would have asked me about our sexual relationship at that stage of marriage, my answer would have been that it was great. We had five years to work on it before we had kids. There were a lot of good things about this time and, as I have written earlier, a lot of struggles, but I think we would both agree that the sexual relationship was good. Other than fights, nothing else was there as a distraction that hindered our sexual relationship. We had the time and the place and the sexual energy. There was the newness, and we were doing a lot of exploring.

If you asked me about our sexual relationship today, I would say it is great, and I am sure Nancy would agree. Yet, when I compare it to the "great" of our first years, there are lots of differences. Today I think we understand the *dod* part of the sexual relationship much better. We always did a pretty good job with the physical part, but God has grown us in the spiritual part. It was not there in the beginning. Maybe the seeds were planted, but I think it was cultivated over the years.

There is a sense of growth and maturity that comes with that mingling of souls. As I look back over the years, I see that area of our marriage had pluses and minuses. Sometimes it was good and sometimes it was just there. As our love for each other continued to grow, sex was not only a physical act we enjoyed but also a deep soul mate connection that is difficult for words to describe. Our experience is this. The sex gets better every year. If you're willing to work at it, I believe this can be true for every married couple.

There are a lot of distractions in marriage, and many of them will affect the sexual relationship. Certainly work is a factor. In our culture today, the majority of couples both work, at least to some extent. Work can add stress to our lives even if we are in a job that we love. Work can leave us tired and with little energy once we get home. So now we have this picture of a couple who comes back from an amazing honeymoon and six months later can barely remember what "good sex" was all about. The side effects of work have taken their toll on the sex life in marriage.

Not only can work distract from the sexual relationship, but kids can also do the same. Most couples want children. Great idea. Great blessing. Big distraction. Kids take time and energy. Are they worth it? Absolutely. But not at the expense of the marriage and the sexual relationship. All too often, I hear the story told of the couple who had this amazing marriage with a great sex life, and then they had two kids in three years and now they hardly connect at all. In reality, if things don't change, they will be a divorce statistic in another couple of years.

Eric and Amanda came through my prep-for-marriage course and attended the same church that we did. They married and had an amazing honeymoon. It was a gift from Amanda's grandfather. Two weeks on a Pacific island at a luxury resort, all expenses covered. It was incredible and they loved every minute of it. They stayed up late and slept in each morning. They ate when they were hungry and spent hours on the beach each day. They connected like never before. Their sexual relationship was amazing, and they enjoyed the freedom marriage gave them.

Before they left for their honeymoon, one of Eric's groomsmen told him if he got bored to call, and he would fly out and play some golf with him. Eric never got bored, and the thought of his friend and golf never crossed his mind. The flight home was full of mixed emotions. They were happy but also sad to see the honeymoon coming to an end. They vowed to each other to keep the feeling going but soon found that life got in the way.

One of the many things that attracted Eric and Amanda to each other was their passion for their work. They were both in jobs they loved, and both were rising stars in their companies. They would celebrate each other's accomplishments and were proud of all they did. One of the things I stressed with them before marriage was the importance of continuing to carve out time for each other daily once they were married. I ran into them almost every week at church, and they looked great and told me all they were doing to build a great marriage. I don't often get to see a couple as they go through that first year of marriage, so I was always excited to keep up with Eric and Amanda.

It was probably close to two months after their first anniversary that I had not seen them at church for a few weeks. I did not think much about it. They could be going to a different service, or I might have just missed running into them. Finally, there they were again and shared the news that they were pregnant and how the first weeks had been rough for Amanda. The pregnancy continued to be pretty difficult, and their first baby was born a few weeks premature but with a good prognosis. It took Amanda quite a while to recover, but she had help both from her mom and Eric's mother. At the end of three months, Amanda was back full time at work, and life moved on for them.

Four years later, Eric and Amanda sat in my office. They had a four-year-old, a three-year-old, and a six-month-old, and they hated each other. As they talked, I realized they had never recovered after their first child. Lots of stress from both jobs, a baby that had a tough first year, a pregnancy that was not planned, and now a third child they had agreed on. The kids took all their time and energy, and they had not invested time in their marriage in a long time. Life had literally swallowed them up and spit them out, and they did not like each other at all.

What happened? Eric and Amanda made choices that hurt

their marriage. During the first pregnancy, Eric had a choice. At work, there was a new project offered to him. He talked about it with Amanda. She was hesitant. She was pregnant and sick and needed him with her. This project would add hours to his week and involved quite a bit of travel. Eric chose the project, and Amanda felt abandoned at the first time she felt she really needed him in their marriage. Amanda was not ready to go back to work after three months off but did so for a number of wrong reasons. Her resentment toward Eric was building.

Then came the unexpected pregnancy, even with Eric using protection and Amanda back on the pill. Amanda's second pregnancy was surprisingly better than the first, but that made no difference in their marriage. After the second baby was born, they made a commitment to each other to get things back on track with their marriage. It was a great idea, but the follow-through never happened. Amanda convinced Eric to have the third child. In her thinking, maybe this would turn things around. It did not, and now they were sitting in my office where they should have sat four years earlier.

Many of you will identify with Amanda and Eric. A lot of us have great honeymoons, and that is awesome, but life is not a honeymoon. Life has a way of bleeding all over our happy marriages. Most of us encounter the birth of kids, stress from jobs, and sickness in our marriages. Each time something arises we have a choice as to how we will handle it. We can work on it together or separately. We can be each other's advocate or adversary. We can work together for a solution or complicate the problem.

Each time something arises we have a choice as to how we will handle it. We can work on it together or separately. We can be each other's advocate or adversary.

The choice is ours. Eric and Amanda entered marriage with a tightly wound knot holding them together that they let unravel completely over a five-year period. Not handling their distractions properly brought them to the point of divorce.

If distractions are a given, how do we handle them in marriage? Nancy and I agree that the greatest blessing God has given us in our marriage is our children, and they have also been the biggest distraction. We did some things right. We consistently carved out time for each other each day, and we had weekly dates built into our schedule. Yet, with all we were doing that was right, we still had a disconnect, and it was totally my fault. We differed on some of the ways we parented, and because I thought I was right, I was not going to give in. Not only did that cause a big disconnect in our marriage, but it also sent a mixed message to our kids.

It took me a long time (way too long) to come around and get on the same team with Nancy as we parented. I knew I was being stubborn but let my pride get the best of me. Once I let go, I think we made up some lost ground, but there was definitely damage done.

There have been other distractions. Some have been big and some small. I think there is seldom a day that passes that we do not have the opportunity to be distracted from our marriage. The key is how we handle the distractions. Always take the time to ask yourself this question, "How will this affect my marriage?" Do you have any idea how much better our marriages would be if we took the time to ask that simple question and think through the answer? If I have a new responsibility at work, how will it affect my marriage? If I play on that softball team, how will it affect my marriage? If I make a certain decision without talking to my spouse, how will it affect my marriage?

You get the idea. Don't let anything distract you from your marriage. Remember, God first, spouse second.

A New Kind of Foreplay

Let's finish this step by looking at this idea. What if we labeled successful foreplay as something that lasted twenty-four hours every day? A 24/7 deal? The foreplay and intimacy I want us to consider here is not overtly sexual in nature but has strong sexual connotations. I believe that great sex is accomplished by a marriage lifestyle that is constantly focusing on foreplay and intimacy. Are you confused? That's okay because this is a little bit different way of thinking about sex. Let me give you an example.

Nancy oversees the running of our home, especially on the inside. If something goes out, she gets the repairman. She is good at this and being in real estate usually knows the best people to call. There are things in the house that she wants to do. Most of them involve cleaning something the way she wants it to be cleaned. No problem. The thing she does not like to do by herself is make the beds. So if I am proactive and offer to help her or, even better, if I make the beds for her, that is foreplay. It is not sexual at all, but it shows love, care, and concern; and that makes her feel loved, and the more she feels loved the more she is drawn to me. If I am consistently every day conscious of things I can do to make her day easier, that is foreplay and builds intimacy.

Do you know what else happens? The more I do for her, the more she does for me. Not that I need the foreplay!

I have told couples for years that in most cases if you do the things that show love and concern for your spouse the other twenty-three-plus hours of the day, the sexual relationship will take care of itself. The greatest sexual organ for a woman is often her mind. As most men think about sex with their wives often, most women make a conscious choice to think about sex. It is just one of those differences that many couples experience. So guys, answer this question. Do you think it will be easier for her to make that choice if you have been attentive to her needs? Ninety-nine percent of the time, the answer will be yes.

What about fights? How do they fit in with this foreplay concept? The answer is easy; they do not. In fact, they can suck a week's worth of foreplay right out of the marriage. I have literally had women tell me that they have been in big fights with their husbands with yelling and screaming and cursing and name calling. Then, not thirty minutes later, their husband wants sex and cannot understand why she is not interested. Part of that is our wiring differences, and part of it is the movies.

How often do we see a couple fight and then immediately embrace in a fit of passion? It's Hollywood's job to sell movies, not to give us an accurate picture of male/female wiring. They seem to do a pretty good job at being consistently inaccurate. The bottom line is that fights, and especially big fights, have nothing to do with foreplay and intimacy.

If fighting is getting in the way of your intimacy, go back a secret or two and review. We'll wait here for you.

Your Turn

Think about it this way. Foreplay and intimacy in your marriage need to be a lifestyle.

What if you consistently put your spouse's needs in front of yours? What if you did everything you could to make their day easier? What if you took a little time out of your workday to text an "I love you" to your spouse? What if you planned a date for the two of you?

If you consistently live your life this way, your sex life in marriage will be better. It may even be a lot better. The only problem I see is if your sole purpose in doing all these things is to have more sex. If it is not a lifestyle change and your heart is not changed, it won't work. Well, it may work for a little while, but it will not last. Trust me, wives know better.

It is amazing how such a simple act as the act of sex can become so complicated. Animals have sex, and they seem to not have the problems we have; but animals do not have a soul. For an animal, the sex act is as good as it gets. For many people the sex act is as good as it gets, but for Christians there is the possibility of *dod*. *Dod* is different.

> *Dod* is like the superglue of sex. It binds us together at a deep level, in a way that words cannot express, and it never lets go.

Dod is like the superglue of sex. It binds us together at a deep level and never lets go. It is the body, mind, and soul of a husband united with the body, mind, and soul of his wife in a way that words cannot express, but the husband and wife know. They both experience it. They may not be able to describe it to others, but they can look at each other and know they have experienced it together.

My challenge to you is to not accept anything less than this in your marriage. Your sexual relationship may need some work. Step one is probably not going to happen in the bedroom. Step one is all about those other twenty-three-plus hours of the day.

> *Ask yourself:*
>
> How do you treat each other? How do you speak to each other? Do you put each other's needs before your own?

Do the 24/7 foreplay. Make it your lifestyle. Then work on the bedroom part. Talk about what you like and do not like. Be adventurous. God has given us a lot to enjoy in each other's bodies. Know that God has given you the sexual relationship in your marriage as a gift. Enjoy and get ready for the rockets!

FIGHT

The Power of Fighting Together on the Same Team

When someone says "I do" for life, it's easy to assume that from then on, that person is on your side. The hard work of pursuit is over, right? Now that there's a ring on his or her finger, you don't have to fight for the heart anymore.

I'm here to tell you, this is not so. The best marriages have lots of fight in them — but it's fighting *together* that makes the difference.

We can do a pretty good job of fighting in our marriage, but that is totally different. Fighting for your marriage means that the two of you are on the same team. You are standing side by side and vow together to never let anything separate the two of you. That is a fight worth having.

If you are married, think back to the days leading up to your wedding. For most of us, that was a time of great anticipation. We were excited about being married. We were in love and knew our marriage would be different. We were going to be the statistics busters. Our marriage would be the love story passed down in our family for generations to come. We could hardly wait to get started. I think most of us identify at least in part with that scenario.

Of all the couples I have married over the years, I have never heard these words as they approached their marriage: "We are going to give this a shot and see if it works out," or "If she just becomes who I want her to be, we will be fine" or "Once I get him to change, we will make it." No. Those are not the things we say on our wedding day, but how many people say them or something similar as they get into their marriage? From looking at the statistics on divorce, over half of us.

How do we get from "I do" to "I don't"? How do some of us get there in only a few weeks or months? Honestly, I guess it doesn't matter when the "I don't" shows up in a marriage. It just bothers me when it shows up early. It troubles me when a couple quits before they even get started. What were they thinking going into marriage? What were their expectations? Why is it seemingly so easy to walk away from something that at one time they wanted so much?

I met Cheryl and Jack in premarital counseling. They had been married a little over one year when Cheryl called me. She wanted the conversation to be brief; she told me that she was leaving Jack and just thought I needed to know. Her words were hard for me to hear. I did not think I would ever get that call from either of them. I asked Cheryl to come by my office to talk. At first reluctant, she finally agreed. As she talked, unfortunately, I heard a familiar story.

Let's go back a little over a year and look at the steps that took Cheryl out of her marriage. Sometimes when I teach a preparing-for-marriage class, a couple will want to see me outside of class for a few counseling sessions. Often, this is because of something that came up in class that they would like to work through. I love doing that with couples and am encouraged that they are proactively taking another step before they take the big step.

Jack and Cheryl were different. They wanted to do counseling in order to further ensure the success of their future marriage. Both were in their late twenties, and this would be the first marriage for each of them.

Jack was bright and personable. In high school, he was a football star as well as valedictorian of his class. He had a few offers to play college ball but chose to focus on his studies and get ready for medical school instead. This proved to be a wise choice, and doors of opportunity kept opening for him. He finished his medical residency and was entering a one-year fellowship program.

Cheryl was also a high school athlete, leading her team to the state soccer championship her senior year. She also had offers to continue her soccer career in college and decided that was the direction she would take. She attended a large university with a great women's soccer program and lots of tradition. She sat on the bench most of her freshman year but earned much more playing time as a sophomore. Midway through her junior season, Cheryl suffered an injury that ended her soccer career forever. It was a devastating blow that shattered a lot of her dreams. The rest of that year she described herself as someone just "going through the motions."

Over the summer, she spent time talking to a number of people she respected. She wanted to see how people viewed her and hopefully get a sense of direction for her future. The result was a determination to attend school to become a physician's assistant. It felt right, and even though she would have to take some classes before applying, this is what she wanted to do. Academically, Cheryl had always been a good student, and the course work was never an issue.

While she was on the medical school campus, she met Jack. It was not love at first sight, but there was definitely an attraction from the beginning. They had mutual friends and spent the early days of their relationship just hanging out together. Time passed, and their relationship grew; finally, in front of all their friends, Jack asked Cheryl to be his wife.

They had been engaged about three months when they attended my class, and it was halfway through the class when they asked to meet with me privately. As they told me their stories, I asked them what they hoped to accomplish through counseling. Their answer was the same. They wanted to do everything they could to make this marriage work, especially since each had come out of a broken home.

I wish I could tell you that I saw the handwriting on the wall with Jack and Cheryl, but I did not. We talked about what the first year of marriage would bring with Jack completing a fellowship and Cheryl continuing to work as a PA. I stressed setting aside time for each other and told them they could not put building their marriage on hold for a year. They seemed to understand and vowed to always make it a priority. We met three times. They completed the class and were married soon after it ended.

Jack's fellowship had been intense and involved long hours each day. They did well the first three or four months but then were not as consistent with their time together. The office Cheryl worked in was expanding and during the expansion was shorthanded. Since Jack was so busy, she opted for longer hours until they could hire another PA. In the last part of the fellowship, another young doctor who had been a year behind him in medical school joined Jack. She was bright and attractive, and Jack seemed to not be as eager to get home as he had in the past.

As far as Cheryl knew, Jack and the new doctor had not been intimate, but she felt him drifting away from her emotionally. It scared her, and she had seen the same thing happen to her mother. Cheryl was determined to not repeat her mother's mistakes. Her mom stayed in the marriage and tried to make it work only to end up in a messy divorce. Cheryl would not let Jack hurt her any more than he had so far.

It was the second time in her life that Cheryl's dreams had been shattered, first with soccer and now with Jack. I asked Cheryl if she thought Jack would talk to me, and she thought he would. After a couple of tries, Jack returned my call and agreed to come into my office.

A different Jack sat on my couch. Gone was the self-confidence, replaced by sadness. The story he shared with me mirrored the one Cheryl told me a week earlier. He told me that he was never intimate with the female doctor in the program with him, but they were emotionally connected. As Cheryl's work became more demanding, Jack found himself spending much more time with his colleague. They not only worked together but also had lunch, dinner, or both together often. He knew it was not right yet did nothing to stop it. Now Cheryl wanted out and repeatedly told him she was done, and she was. On the day of their eighteen-month anniversary, Jack and Cheryl were officially divorced.

For me, this was a tough case. First, I liked them both and knew they worked hard to keep this from happening as they prepared for marriage. Even though they had been determined to break the divorce cycle in their families, they added another notch on the belt instead.

Second, I questioned myself. What did I miss? Could I have helped them prevent this from happening? Lots of questions — few answers. The situation Jack and Cheryl found themselves in was similar to the situations many couples find themselves in. They prepare for marriage and have high hopes of success, and then one choice turns everything upside down.

Jack repeated their family histories. He did the same thing his father did to his mother and Cheryl's dad did to her mother. Jack took a step toward another woman when he should have taken a step toward Cheryl. Instead of coming to Cheryl and saying, "I feel like we are drifting apart, and I am having feelings of vulnerability that scare me," Jack told her nothing and continued to drift away. Jack had a chance to fight for his marriage but did not, and now it was over. He told me all the things he would do differently if he could get a do over. Fighting for your marriage is doing all those things the first time. Often the second time is too late. It was for Jack.

Even though Jack took the steps that eventually led him out of their marriage, Cheryl was not willing to fight for her marriage. The risk of pain was too great for her. I talked to her about hope and what I knew God could do if she would give Him and Jack a chance. The chance scared her, and her life experiences told her shattered dreams were shattered forever. I think she wanted to believe God could heal this mess, but it was a hill she was not willing to climb. She chose not to fight for her marriage.

Earlier I defined fighting for your marriage as being on the same team and not letting anything come between the two of you. Jack and Cheryl started marriage on the same team. They were aware of some of the obstacles they would face and were unaware of others. Work began to separate them, and they let it. Nobody said, "There is a problem here." Nobody said, "We are moving from one team to two." Nobody said, "We are treading on treacherous ground." Nobody said anything.

If you were Jack or Cheryl, what would you have done? What would you do if something were coming between you and your spouse? Would you fight for your marriage or just keep on keeping on? The decisions we make in these situations will either bring life or death to our marriages. Never forget that you have a choice.

The Marriage That Wins Together

Maybe I made some assumptions in talking to you about fighting for your marriage. Maybe you do not see marriage as worth fighting for. After all, you can always find another person to marry. Fighting for your marriage takes a lot of work, and you may not want to work that hard. From the divorce statistics, it looks like over half the couples who marry come to these conclusions.

Marriage is like playing a slot machine. Every once in a while someone hits the jackpot, but most of us stay there awhile, invest a little time and money, and then move on. But what if every marriage hit a jackpot? Do you think that is a possibility? I do. I really do.

I see couples who stand together no matter what. It is like they are superglued side by side. Life may hit them hard, even knock them down; but they stand together, take the knocks together, and stand together again. It is both a conviction and a mind-set. There is no plan B. And when there is no plan B, you plan to fight harder.

A shining example of winning together, Justin and Heather just celebrated twenty-five years of marriage. That is an incredible accomplishment today. I love this couple and value their friendship. At their celebration party, I overheard a number of comments:

"They have the perfect marriage." "They have had such an easy life together." "Their kids are such a blessing to them." Nice things to say, but these simplistic conclusions made me want to scream.

Why is it that when we see a happy couple, we assume they have had a perfect life, never having to deal with any hardship? This kind of togetherness does not simply happen—it is hard-won. In fact, I have never met a couple with a good marriage who have not gone through hard times. The difference is that some couples go through the hardships superglued together, and some go through them taking separate paths. In other words, some people fight for their marriage and some do not.

Justin and Heather had been married when Justin was twenty, Heather was nineteen, and their daughter was one. Justin was in his first semester of college and Heather was a senior in high school when Heather called Justin to tell him she was pregnant. Justin's happy-go-lucky world turned upside down in one phone call. His first thoughts were for himself. What will my parents think? How could I support a family? How much does an abortion cost?

Heather on the other hand was just scared. Her dad was rough on her as his only daughter and had warned her repeatedly what he would do if she ever had sex before marriage. Now what would he do if he found out she was pregnant?

Justin picked Heather up, and they went to a secluded place to talk. Heather cried for almost two hours. Justin was the guy who always had an answer, but today he had none. It was no easy choice, but they decided to get an abortion. Justin had a part-time job and was saving extra money for his college expenses. He would dip into that fund and pay the doctor or clinic, or whatever.

Heather reluctantly agreed. She hated the thought of abortion but saw no other way for them. They made the appointment for the following Saturday morning. Heather confided in a friend and would stay that afternoon and night with her.

Justin picked her up the next morning, and Heather's parents thought they were going to just have a day together. They were sitting in the doctor's reception room and neither dared speak. It was when the nurse called Heather's name that Justin grabbed her hand and looked into her eyes. "Heather, if you do not want to do this, we will figure it out. I have no answers, but I will be there with you every step." They had barely talked about marriage, and Justin was already fighting for it.

Nicole was born about eight months later. Justin was by Heather's side as their parents waited outside in the hallway. They talked about marriage but decided to take it a step at a time. They didn't want to rush into something and end up hating each other and divorced. Heather left the hospital with Nicole and lived with her parents. Justin continued in school, traded his part-time job for a full-time one, and spent as much time with Heather and Nicole as he could.

During that year they grew their relationship by learning to put God first. They were parenting well together, and their love for each other grew almost daily. Justin popped the question, and they were married a few months later. Most people do not do the math, and I was one of only a few at the twenty-fifth anniversary party who knew the story.

A second child was born three years later—a boy they named Samuel. Samuel was premature and spent the first three months of his life in NICU. It was a roller-coaster ride. One day they received encouraging news and the next, things would change. They were both in the unit the day Samuel's heart stopped beating. They stood by, helpless, as they watched doctors and nurses struggle to bring him back. Samuel survived that scare; miraculously, the tests did not indicate any brain damage at all.

Through those three months of emotional chaos, Justin and Heather stood together. One of the nurses told them early on the toll this situation could take on their marriage. She had seen it time and time again. Justin and Heather were determined to fight through this together, and they did.

Justin was in his dream job. Heather was now a stay-at-home

mom, and the kids were six and ten. Life was good until the company Justin worked for lost a big contract. He knew there would probably be cutbacks but never thought that he would be one of them. The severance package gave them ninety days' breathing room. Surely he would find a job before the money ran out.

Surely did not happen, and nine months of unemployment caused drastic changes in their life. The new home they built and lived in for two years was now someone else's. Nicole and Samuel were no longer in private school. Heather never finished college but found a job where she could work while the kids were in school. The pay was not great, but it helped. Justin was depressed, and each day was a struggle. He heard the word "no" so many times that he never expected to hear anything else. It was a full eleven months before Justin got a job. It was a good job, and they gradually began to rebuild their financial lives.

From the day Justin received notice that he would lose his job until the day he walked into his new job, Heather never said a negative word to him. What they were facing was not his fight. It was their fight, and they fought it together. During a time of crisis when many marriages crash, theirs grew. Justin set the precedent years earlier when Heather was pregnant, and Heather picked right up where he left off.

Over the next few years there were trials, but nothing on the scale of Samuel and the job loss. There were some extended-family issues, some financial problems, and normal struggles with raising two kids. It did not matter what Justin and Heather faced, their plan was the same. They faced it together. There was no finger pointing or blaming. There was only one team, and they were it. They identified the problem, sought God's guidance, and began to fight together.

Do you know what they realized? This is big, and I don't want you to miss it. Here it is: *They realized that no matter what the outcome, when they were fighting together, their marriage always won.*

Isn't that awesome? Isn't that incredible? Here is another

secret. That principle they discovered is universal. That means what worked for them will work for you. If the two of you join together and fight together, your marriage will always win. Always!

God's Way to Fight for Your Marriage

I have this list of why I think marriage is worth fighting for. Granted, it is my list and gleaned from the life experiences of my marriage, but maybe some of the items will fit you.

I read a lot of articles that reflect the way our culture looks at marriage. One recent article talked of the pluses of couples just living together and never getting married. They interviewed couples living that lifestyle, and all were perfectly happy. Other articles encourage those who are married and unhappy to get out. Don't waste time in something that is making you unhappy. If you have a nontraditional stance on marriage, there is probably at least one article out there to back you up.

My issue with most of these articles is that they do not talk about the downside of these choices. Cohabitation statistics are not very good. According to the *Journal of Marriage and the Family*, couples who cohabit have a divorce rate that is 50 percent higher than those who do not.[1] I know there are those today who would challenge these statistics. That's fine. I really do not want or need to fight that battle.

My point is simple. There is only one foolproof plan that works long term for male/female relationships. That is a marriage where every day the couple puts God first and their spouse second. Over the centuries, marriage has taken a lot of hits, but it is still around. God created marriage. God has a plan for marriage. God's plan works best.

Let me give you a premise. Take a couple that marries and does it their way. No God-first and spouse-second deal. Just marriage

---

1. Susan Brown and Alan Booth, "Cohabitation Versus Marriage: A Comparison of Relationship Quality," *Journal of Marriage and the Family* 58 (1996): 669.

on their terms. Maybe it is modeled off the marriage of their parents, or a TV show, or a movie. It does not matter. What I see happen over time is that something else becomes more important to one or both of them than each other or their marriage. In other words, they become first and put something else second. When that happens and things stay that way, the marriage crumbles. They may not divorce, but the marriage has lost its value.

There are a lot of sad things that can accompany a marriage like that, but do you know what I think is the saddest? I think the saddest thing is that they will never experience what Justin and Heather experienced. They will never fight through hardships and come out on the other side. They will never know what benefits come from fighting for their marriage. They will never know the joys of celebrating twenty-five years of marriage still glued tightly together as one.

I think so many people do not understand why Nancy and I have the marriage today that we have. We had so many times that we could have given up. We could have quit and never looked back. Before kids, we could have divorced and never had to see each other again. After kids, we could have divorced and put up with each other till the kids were grown and then only had to see each other at certain life events. Yet if we chose either of those paths, we would never have known what we were going to miss. Sure, today we have battle scars, but each one represents a victory.

God taught us that by honoring the commitment we made together before Him, He would not only be with us through everything we encountered but also would bless us richly. I know. That sounds like church-speak.

Let me say it this way. When we had problems, God showed up. He always does, and He will for you, too. I cannot explain it any other way. We had answers that had to come from Him. When we prayed and sought His help, He always came through. It did not always happen the way I thought it would, but it was always good for us and our marriage—the blessings part. Nancy and I are more in love today than ever. God taught us that love is a verb—an action word. He taught us how to "love one another." He taught us how to be generous and how to share what we have with others. He helped raise our children. He taught us how to live with little and with more. He taught us the importance of fighting for our marriage.

Every couple I have ever talked to that has been married a significant number of years doing marriage God's way says the same thing. They would not trade the scars for anything. They cherish the marriage they have today because they fought for their marriage. If you are just married or have been married for quite some time, begin today to fight together for your marriage and see what God will do.

Peter and Carolyn had six children. They were married for eleven years when I met them. The kids ranged from age ten to six months. Peter and Carolyn basically hated each other. It was a little hard for me to comprehend because they said they had hated each other for years. I was thinking that they had either called a truce six times in their marriage, or they liked sex more than they liked to hate each other. That was one of those questions that I never got a chance to ask.

They were at war with one another. Each had their arsenal of ammunition to throw at the other. Each thought they were right and the other absolutely wrong. Each was always on the defensive and picked apart everything the other said. They were in a huge mess, and I was not sure why they were in my office. So I asked that question. I should have guessed the answer.

Peter wanted me to tell Carolyn to change, and Carolyn wanted me to tell Peter to change. I gave them an alternative. Why don't we see what it would take from both of you to make your marriage better? They both agreed, but I knew they would continue to push their own agendas.

As we talked, I asked another question: "Why do you want your marriage to be better?" They both agreed that they wanted it better for their kids. I could work with that. I see the fallout of divorce all the time. It can be devastating on kids. I knew that in the big picture they needed to be in the marriage for each other, but I could start with the kids as motivation. If a couple stays in the marriage just for the sake of the kids, it is somewhat honorable but has a big built-in fallacy. One day the kids grow up and leave. Then you are left with two strangers who never connected and have no purpose for their marriage. So the kids are grown and the parents divorce and nobody has a place to come home to.

My goal with Peter and Carolyn was to use the motivation of a better marriage for the kids to help them build a marriage that was kid-proof. The process was slow, but gradually Peter and Carolyn were able to turn all that energy they were using to fight each other and together focus it on fighting for their marriage. Today their kids are still at home but a lot closer to adulthood than when we began talking. The marriage is not perfect, but I believe they will not only make it but will also have a marriage that thrives because Peter and Carolyn fought for their marriage and won.

> ### *Think about this question:*
>
> What are your reasons for fighting for your marriage? These are just a few of the ones I see as valuable from a counselor's viewpoint. There are probably as many reasons as there are couples. The bottom line is this: fight for your marriage because there is nothing better in God's creation than a marriage with Him at the center. That was His plan all along. Do not settle for anything less. Fight together for your marriage.

Fighting Together to Be Debt-Free

As you think about your own marriage, what is it you're really fighting about, anyway? There may be many reasons, but studies consistently illuminate one above the rest.

Consider these: we already know that money management is

one of the top dividing issues for couples today. The problems most of us have with money have to do with how we handle our money. I have seen couples on a minimal fixed income make it and have no debt. Some even save a little. I have seen couples who make a lot of money whose debt is almost insurmountable. Debt is a part of our culture, and it is also a marriage killer. Debt brings stress, and many couples go into attack mode when stressed, and they usually end up attacking each other. This is not good.

Carl and Alice married the second week of June after both graduating from college in May. Both had new jobs and both had promising futures. They debated the pros and cons of buying a house for months, but a wedding gift from Alice's grandparents covered the down payment of the house they both wanted. After a week-long honeymoon, they began to settle into their new home. It was a pretty cool house and just needed a little paint to get in shape. Carl and Alice received a number of awesome wedding gifts, which they unpacked and put up in their home. They loved their home and their time together in it.

Life was good until they were invited to a couple's house for dinner one evening. On the outside the house was similar to theirs, but on the inside it was night and day. Their friends' furniture and TV and stereo system and grill and everything were "Wow!" That night Carl and Alice did not say much as they returned home and got ready for bed, but each was thinking, "How can we get some of those things?"

As often happens, credit card companies find new college graduates and offer them lines of credit. They make it sound like the thing to do, and they make it so easy. In this household there was not one but two college grads, and the number of credit card offers just doubles. Who cares if Alice's were in her maiden name? Together they now had over $25,000 in credit.

Problem solved. The shopping was fun. New couch and chairs in the living room plus a few accessories. Carl got the TV he wanted. It was a huge screen and had all the latest features and accessories, including a sound system to die for. Inevitably, you know when you redo one room, it just makes the others look worse; so they went from room to room till everything was redone. They even had some credit left over. Unused credit. Can you imagine that?

You know where this story is going. You have either been there or know someone who has been there. Carl and Alice were overextended in a big way. They could barely pay the credit card minimums along with their other bills. Then came the crowning achievement. Another couple who were their friends invited them to go on a Caribbean cruise. There was just enough credit left on the last card to cover the trip, and off they went. It was a great trip, and they returned home to a life of poverty.

You know the problem with new stuff? It becomes old stuff. The newest TV is outdated, sometimes in months. For Carl and Alice, the new was wearing off quickly and they were stuck at home. There was no extra money for anything. As they looked at their credit card bills together, there was no answer. If they continued making just the minimum payments, they would not pay them off in their lifetimes! Then they took the next logical step for many people. They began to blame each other. Welcome to the world of debt.

Debt, especially debt that you have no way of repaying, is a marriage killer. Have no doubt about it. Debt will get you fighting. Unfortunately, it will get you and your spouse fighting *against* each other, not fighting *for* your marriage.

Here is a novel idea on handling debt. Don't. Fight off the temptation to incur debt at step one. Do not go there. It does not matter how much better you think your life will be with that purchase if you go into debt to have it. We can rationalize almost anything, and if we need help, there are plenty of salespeople who can assist you.

One of you may be weaker than the other in this area. Stay glued together. Don't go off on your own and buy something. Fight this as a team. If you are both weak, you will have a bigger battle, but fight it together. Do you know what would be cool?

What if you both went together and priced that new couch or new TV or new whatever. Then what if you together began to save for it? (I know this is revolutionary, and I wish it was my idea, but it's not. I read that a long time ago people had to pay cash for everything they bought. What an interesting idea!) Once you save the money, go together and buy what you wanted. Guess what happens next? Nothing. No bill in the mail. No stress. No fight over debt.

If you are not in debt, fight together and stay out of debt. If you are in debt, quit fighting each other and get help and a plan and fight the debt together until it is completely gone, and then fight together to never go there again.

When the Fight Gets Hard

You will have many, many opportunities in your marriage to break your commitments to each other. You will be put on the spot to compromise your relationship, and when you are, you have a choice. Choose to fight for your marriage—no matter the cost.

Bruce and Judith were faced with this situation. Bruce worked for the same company for five years and finally was given a chance to advance. With the advance came a good pay increase, a different job focus, and some travel. Bruce and Judith were excited and grateful for the opportunity. Bruce's schedule changed some, and now there were some dinner meetings. For the first few months Bruce's boss accompanied him on these dinners. These were business-focused but involved a few drinks, and all the conversation was not centered on business. Bruce was learning the ropes and liked the process. A dinner was set for Bruce, his boss, and their newest client, who was a single woman about Bruce's age.

Bruce left the office a little early to stop by the house and change clothes. As he headed for the restaurant, his boss called him. His flight was delayed and he would not make the dinner. He told Bruce he trusted him and knew he would do a great job. Bruce pulled his car over to the side of the road. He was not worried about handling the client. He was worried about Judith.

One of the commitments they made to each other involved not having lunch or dinner with someone of the opposite sex. It seemed kind of silly in today's culture, but both agreed it was important. Meals between two people of different sexes can be intimate. Throw in a few drinks, and it could get very intimate.

Bruce made a call on the fly. He would talk to Judith about it later.

Bad call on the fly. Yes, he was trapped, but in hindsight, a call to tell her the situation would have helped a lot. Instead, she was upset about the dinner and felt deceived by his omission.

Now they sat in my office dealing with two issues—what had happened and what might happen in the future. Bruce knew this was just the beginning of the dinners and possible trips with members of the opposite sex. Before he was promoted, he often heard some of the guys talking about what they did on their trips and some of the women they met at dinner. He kept those at a distance, but now he was in the same boat with the other guys.

I told them there were probably some options for them, but they had to fight together. This could not divide them. They both agreed, and then Judith said something that amazed me. She turned to Bruce and said, "I trust you. This is not going to come between us. You can do what you need to do in your job." Bruce teared up. The session ended, and we set a time to meet the following week.

They came back with a plan and they wanted my input. Bruce made the decision that he would not and could not violate the commitment he made to Judith. That meant no dinners with women alone and no trips with women alone. If it cost him his job, he was okay with that. He had an appointment the following morning at 9:00 a.m. to talk to his boss. We prayed together, asking God to give Bruce the perfect words to say and his boss to really hear what Bruce was saying.

The next day around noon, Bruce called me. I could tell by the tone of his voice that things were good. I just did not know the details. Bruce said his boss listened, contemplated what he said, and then asked a few questions. He wanted to know how Bruce would handle the dinners, and Bruce told him he would just invite another colleague to come along. He would like to handle trips the same way. Bruce told me that his boss sat silent for what seemed like a long time and then looked Bruce in the eyes and said, "Okay. We will try it your way."

I know every boss would not react the way Bruce's did, but that is not the point. The point is that Bruce and Judith fought for their marriage. They chose not to compromise. They went countercultural. Since the boss said yes, we have a happy ending, but even if he said no, we still would have had a happy ending.

Are you facing something that could hurt your marriage? Is there something in your job or with the friends you hang out with? Is the world telling you something is okay while your heart is screaming no? Here is what I would like for you to take away from this story. Never let anything cause you to compromise your marriage. Never hide anything from your spouse. Lay everything out on the table, discuss it together and come up with a plan, and stand side by side in implementing it. In this process, unlike Bruce, you might lose your job, but you will never lose your marriage.

The Real Number One Enemy

At this point, I have to tell you something that I've been dreading telling you since page one of the book. This is one of the biggest culprits I see get in between a husband and a wife, and I am fully guilty of it. Honestly, it is probably the number one problem most of us deal with today. It certainly is for me.

Here's the truth: I am a selfish person. Over and over again in all our years of marriage, I have struggled not to let my selfishness come between Nancy and me. It started early in marriage when I wanted to get my way at the expense of Nancy not going to her friend's wedding in Fort Worth, and it has continued to be something I fight almost every day. When I am selfish, I am only concerned about one thing, and that is me. "Me" can take over both position one and position two in my life. Instead of God being first, I am first. Instead of Nancy being second, I put myself ahead of her.

This is where the fighting in marriage gets personal, because to fight for your marriage you have to fight against yourself.

I know from experience that my life runs best when God runs it. He always looks out for my best interest. His plan is far better than mine. He loves me more than anyone else does. I know all that, but there are times when I make the decision to do it my way. I think I know what is best for me, and I know the plan to make it happen, and no one will watch out for me like I do. How do I go from God first to me first?

From a spiritual viewpoint, it is my sin nature. Even though I have been a Christian for a number of years, there are times when I take God out of the driver's seat of my life. I want to do it my way. A contributing factor is the fact that my way seems to work for a while. Often there is no immediate pain. The consequences are coming, but they are in the future. Today I feel no pain. Ultimately things crash, and I ask myself the same questions over and over again. Why did I think my way would work? Why did I think my way would be better than God's way? Why can't I just trust God and follow His lead? Actually, I am better than I used to be. I have learned from my experiences.

Leaving my life in His hands is not only the right thing to do but also the smart thing to do. But every once in a while that doubt comes in the back of my mind and I begin to wonder if my plan might just be a little better than God's. Then is the time that I need to catch that doubt in its infancy before it has a chance to grow. The truth is that no matter how brilliant I think my plan is or how strong the temptation is to stray from God's path for my life, nothing compares day after day to putting Him first.

This may not be revolutionary to you, but I have found that when I put God first and keep Him first, it is a lot easier to put

Nancy second. If I were following His plan for my life, who would He want me to put in the number two position? The Bible tells us to seek God first and everything else will be added to us (Matthew 6:33). I do not think that is just a principle to live out. I think it is a promise from God. Seek Him with everything you have. Pursue Him relentlessly, and then watch how everything else falls into place.

Selfishness rears its head in our marriage when I am out of balance with God. It is those times when I think of my needs, wants, and desires first. Actually, I think of them first, second, third, and so on. Nancy asks me to help her with a project. I am watching TV. It does not matter what I am watching or whether I am interested in it or not. The issue is that she is stepping into my world and interrupting me, and my answer to her is "No."

We are going out to dinner, and I drive to my restaurant of choice without asking her opinion, which I do not want to hear anyway. We are headed to a game, and on the way we pass one of her favorite stores. She wants to stop for a few minutes, but I say no because I might miss watching the team warm up. I am in the last part of the book I have been reading as she comes into the room. She sits down and says she would like to spend some time with me. At first I ignore her, and when that does not work, I say, "After I finish the book." If I am into myself, all those scenarios can become reality, but if I am into God, things play out differently. I will help her with the project and ask where she would like to go to dinner and stop at her favorite store and lay the book down.

Every day I have choices like this to make. One is for me and one is for us. If I am living God's way, us always wins and me always loses.

So how do we need to fight against selfishness? We fight it just like we fight everything else. We fight it together, and I believe this is our greatest battle. We must fight together to keep God first when almost everything we encounter each day tells us to turn a different direction.

That is why it is so important for a couple to attend church together and read the Bible together and to pray together. That's how we fight selfishness. We never give it a foothold. We never turn in that direction. Instead we plant God firmly at the center of our lives and our marriage. That transforms us. That breaks down walls and builds an unshakable foundation. That is fighting together for your marriage.

Your Turn

Picture a boxing ring. It is elevated and not that big. It is surrounded by ropes linked together at the four corners. Seated around the ring is the crowd. They are yelling and cheering and saying some unprintable things. In the middle of the ring are only two people—the boxers. There is no referee. Above the ring is a list of the rules for the boxers. The rules talk about fighting fair and what can and cannot be done, but there is no one there to enforce them. No one is there to protect one boxer from the other or to prevent one boxer from breaking the rules. Make your way to the ring so you can get a close-up of the boxers. Now you see something strange. One boxer is a man and the other is a woman.

They square off, each staring at the other. Someone, somewhere rings a bell and the fight begins. If you were a betting person, you would bet on the man. He is bigger and appears to be much stronger than the woman, but as the fight progresses, she stands her ground well and lands some powerful punches of her own. In a regular boxing match there are rounds. The boxers fight for a few minutes, and then the bell rings again, and they get a minute or so to separate and to rest. Then they go another round and repeat the process until someone wins.

This fight is different. There are no rounds, and the bell does not ring again. This is a one-round fight to the finish. The boxers continue to trade punches. Some are fair and some are not, but there is no one to judge the fight. As it continues, both boxers are a mess. They are tired, beat-up, and running out of fight.

Finally it ends. It is hard to tell if there is a winner as both boxers walk away. Someone tells you the boxers are married, or were. As you look at the ring, you see something lying on the floor. It is a piece of paper. You climb in the ring and pick up the piece of paper. Now it makes sense. Now you know what you just witnessed. That boxing match was their marriage, and the piece of paper is their divorce decree. The boxer husband did not win and neither did the boxer wife. The winner is the piece of paper you hold in your hand. The crowd leaves in silence as they have just witnessed a death.

But what if it didn't have to be this way?

Take the same picture. Same boxing ring, same crowd, same husband and wife boxers. They stand in the middle of the ring facing each other. Someone rings a bell. Then a strange thing happens as the husband and wife boxers turn and stand side by side and join hands and walk around the ring daring anyone to challenge them.

As they make their way around the ring, you notice they have been joined by Someone. This Someone is not there to fight against them, He is there to fight with them on their side. Challengers climb into the ring, but they are no match for the three. One by one the challengers are defeated. The husband and wife boxers seem to be gaining strength. The fights are not tiring them. They are energized and rejuvenated. It is time for you to go, but you leave knowing the boxers and their Friend are going to be okay. There will be no divorce decree here. The fight may go on, but the boxers are fine, and you are confident they will continue to defeat each challenger they face.

Now put those two boxing rings side by side. Both are now empty. Take your spouse and approach the rings. Which one will you enter? It is your choice. Enter ring one and fight against each other till your marriage dies, or enter ring two and fight together with God for the rest of your lives. I don't know about you, but I choose ring two. I am going to stand with Nancy and God and fight together with them for my marriage. Now that's fighting the good fight. That is a marriage that wins.

A FINAL WORD

Imagine a new couple on their wedding day. They are filled with hope, anticipation, and excitement at all the days to come. No newlyweds think to themselves, *I hope in a few years we end up in a hot mess.* Or, *I can't wait to run our love dry and for everything to fall apart.* As a counselor, I can promise you: no one gets married thinking about divorce. No one hopes this will happen to him or her. Divorce is for "those other people," not them.

I know because I thought this, too. As far as I knew, there had never been a divorce in either side of my family as far back as I could trace. I took that for granted, along with the idea that my marriage would just fall in place with the long line of marital successes.

Then reality hit, and it hit hard. People other than "those other people" got divorced, and I was afraid that I was going to be one of them. That scared me a lot. It was not just being the first in my family to go to divorce court that scared me, although that was a factor. It was also the thought of living the rest of my life without the person I promised to live the rest of my life with. That was scary. I knew there had to be a way not only to save my marriage but also to build something that would be special to both of us. At a time in my life that I needed a miracle, I turned to the Miracle Worker.

My belief is in a God who created marriage and who has a perfect plan for each marriage. That includes yours. Every day will not be great, but God will take the good and the bad and make something beautiful out of it. Marriage is persevering. It is staying on that marriage highway with your eyes focused on Him. All the things you encounter will either draw you to an exit or draw you closer to Him. Stay on the highway.

I would like to tell you that the highway at some point will smooth out, and at times it does, but if we only live for the smooth road, we miss a lot. Most of what God has taught Nancy and me has not come on smooth roads. The times that have drawn us closer to each other and to Him have usually come over the roughest of terrain.

While going through those times, I would have given almost anything to have them end. Yet looking back at them now, I see their value in our marriage and would not change anything. It's funny how those rough times that we hate can become the past times that we cherish. If you asked me the one thing I have learned from marriage, it would be that whatever the problem, there is always an answer.

Some of you are reading this book from the south side of divorce. You may be thinking you blew it, and God will never give you another chance at marriage. Take some solace in the knowledge that all of us have blown it. Sure, the Bible says that "God hates divorce." And He does hate it, for all the same reasons that it brings pain to those it touches. But the Bible never says that God hates divorced people. Our God is about forgiveness and new beginnings.

When God gives you that new beginning, be ready. Prepare well and learn from your past. Be determined to break bad cycles and do marriage God's way. If you do, your next marriage will be incredibly awesome.

Now you know the Seven Secrets, and they are no longer secrets. It's time to make a shift from "secrets" to "steps." If all you do is read this book and lay it down and walk away, nothing will change. You will have a head full of ideas that will gradually be replaced by other things, and sometime in the future you will realize nothing in your marriage has changed, and it may have even gotten worse. On the other hand, you can together make a plan to walk through these seven steps together. Here are ideas to help you get started.

Step One — STOP

Together, identify the cycles you are in as a couple that are unhealthy and need to be broken. They may come from your family of origin, your culture, or from your life together. Once you identify them, decide what you need to do to STOP. Both of you will play a part in this process no matter where the cycle began. You may decide to involve a Christian counselor or a pastor for guidance and accountability. Remember, if you don't get step one under control, it will limit your progress in all of the other steps.

Step Two — START

Pursue God together. The best thing about this step is that God is ready and waiting for you. He is so excited to be invited into the fabric of your marriage. He has a plan for your marriage that is much more incredible than you could ever imagine. Read the Bible together, pray together, serve together, and worship together. Put God first and keep Him there.

Step Three — CONNECT

There is no shortcut to spending time together. Look at the three areas of compassion, authenticity, and empathy. How would you rate yourself in relation to your spouse in each of these areas? What can you do to improve? Work on listening and use STOP-LOOK-LISTEN until it becomes a regular part of your conversation together.

Step Four — ENGAGE

Practice being open and honest with each other. Resolve issues and leave them in the past. Don't judge your spouse. Choose your battles well. Begin using our five-step method to resolve problems. Agree together to use the "Time-Out" in your marriage, and then use it! You put God first in step two. Make sure nothing is ever in second place except your spouse. Especially watch where you put stuff, family and friends, expectations, and addictions. Remember to see your spouse through God's eyes, and never let go of the hopes and dreams God has planted in your marriage.

Step Five — BALANCE

How much space does time with God and time with your spouse get on your pie chart? How would you rate the quality of the time you spend with God and with your spouse? Is your spouse your best friend? If not, do one thing today to begin that process. What do you do as a couple for fun? When is the last time you had fun together? If you are doing well in this area, keep it up. If not, plan a fun date. Get in the habit of going over your schedules together each week and make sure they have balance. What traditions do you have as a couple? Is it time to begin a new one? Finally, are you financially balanced? If not, decide your first step together and then follow through.

Step Six — MINGLE

Do you see the sexual relationship in marriage as a gift from God? If not, what is blocking you? Don't let anything stand in the way of receiving this gift. Discuss the different needs of a husband and a wife that affect the sexual relationship. How can you come alongside of each other in meeting these needs? Share with each other what you think is romantic. Then be romantic! There are no shortcuts to a great sexual relationship. It takes time, effort, and sacrifice, but the results are incredible and will build a closeness you will not experience in any other way.

Step Seven — FIGHT

You will either stand together and fight for your marriage or stand apart and fight against each other. Don't ever forget that if you fight together, your marriage will always win. This is a simple choice. Two choices. Two ways you could go. One breathes life into your marriage while the other sucks the life out of your marriage. If you choose to fight each other, you might as well throw the towel in today. Your marriage will not survive. If you choose to fight together, you will see your marriage grow each day, each week, and each year.

———

That's it. Now you know all the secrets. There's only one catch — they will do absolutely nothing for your marriage *unless you put them to work*. To work, you have to turn these seven secrets into seven steps, and invite your spouse to do the same.

Go through the process together, and you will build something so special that nothing can tear it apart. You will have the marriage God intended for you to have. You will have hope like you never had before. You will have intimacy at its deepest level. You will have an awesome marriage.

ACKNOWLEDGMENTS

Thanks to everyone who has added words of encouragement along the way.

I am so thankful for these people that God put in my life:

The late Jim Morris, who convinced me to write.

Chris Hudson, who has been a great editor, agent, and friend.

My Zondervan Team:
David Morris, who really believed in this book from the beginning.
Alicia Kasen and the entire marketing team.
All my editors, John Sloan, Stephanie Smith, and Jim Ruark. Words cannot really express how much you have meant to me.

My Awesome Marriage Team:
Tanner Herriot, who is a master at telling stories through video.
Andy Knight, who makes our website great.
Nils Smith, who is my social media guru.
You guys are the best!

To my grandkids, who never let my closed office door stop them from coming in!

Most of all, to Nancy, who has walked this road with me. You are truly the love of my life, my best friend, and my "dod" mate!